# Sukhoi Fitters in action

## By Hans-Heiri Stapfer

**Color by Don Greer**
**Illustrated by Perry Manley**

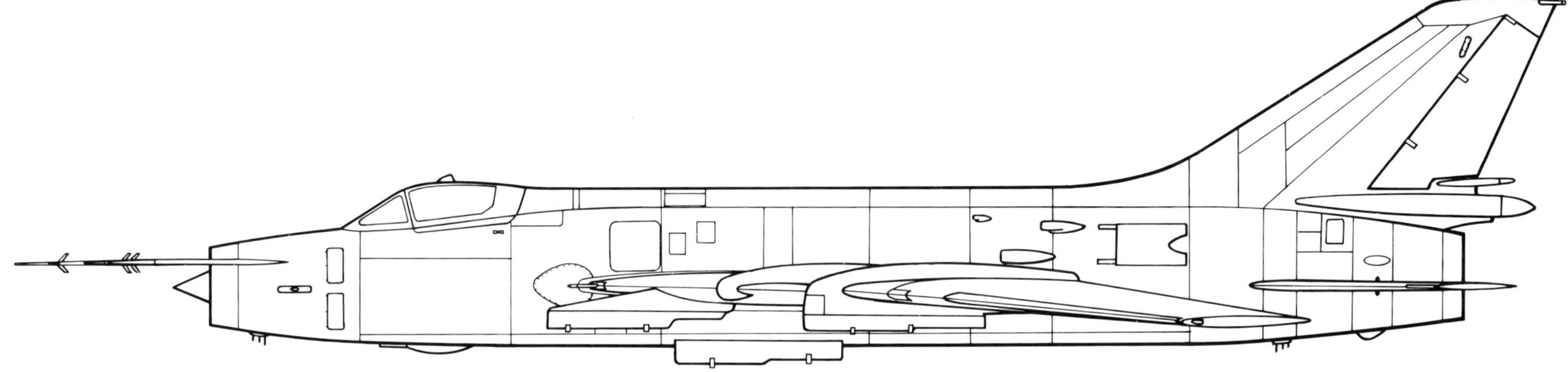

**Aircraft Number 90**
squadron/signal publications

On 19 August 1981, in what became known world-wide as the Gulf of Sidra Incident, a pair of Libyan Arab Air Force Su-22M-2 Fitter Js engaged two F-14A Tomcats of VF-41 over the Gulf of Sidra. The lead Fitter fired an AA-2 Atoll missile at the F-14s, which missed its target. The F-14s returned fire with AIM-9 Sidewinder missiles, destroying both Fitters.

# Editor's Note

The name Fitter is not actually part of the Soviet designation of the Su-7. Fitter is, in fact, a reporting name; that is, a name assigned to the aircraft by the North Atlantic Treaty Organization's Air Standards Coordinating Committee, a joint committee made up of members from all member countries. The purpose of these reporting names is to allow rapid radio identification/reporting of Soviet aircraft types. The names are all designed to sound different so that they will not be confused, even under conditions of poor radio reception.

Single syllable names are used for propeller-driven aircraft, while multiple syllable names are used for jet-powered aircraft. The name also gives the basic mission of the aircraft. Names beginning with B are for bombers; transports all begin with C; helicopters with H; and miscellaneous types (trainers, reconnaissance, etc) begin with M.

Fighter aircraft all have names beginning with F; therefore, under the NATO Reporting Name System, the Su-7 was named Fitter indicating that it is a jet-powered fighter aircraft. Variants of the basic aircraft are all identified by a suffix letter. The second Su-7 variant, identified by NATO, would receive the name Fitter B; the third, Fitter C, etc. Often this does not follow actual Soviet production, since a type may actually be a third production variant, and be identified/named by NATO before the second production variant was seen by NATO observers.



# Dedication

This book is dedicated to a number of interesting people who have entered my life over the past few years. People, like my beer drinking friends, who seem to always invade my home just when I need complete silence to finish the book; especially Chris, Alfie, Fuesi, Stuker, Lauber, Pete, and Werni. Then there are the Tax Sharks of the Inland Revenue Office at Horgen; the lazy girls at the Horgen Post Office who always become angry if you bring in more than two letters to be stamped and mailed; and finally the countless numbers of Eastern European modelers whose loyalty to their socialist governments and the communist ideal ends when there are Western kits and publications available for trade. Life would be so boring without all of you.

# Photo Credits

Robert Bock
Robert J. Ruffle Archives
Don Henry
William White
Sebastian Aeroflop
WTD-61 (Erprobungstelle Manching)

Inter-Photo-Agency
U.S. Navy
Nicholas J. Waters III
B.G.K. Pictures
Auen Wolpertinger
The Molotov Cocktail Gang

Polish Air Force pilots head for debriefing while ground crews begin servicing their Su-22M-4 Fitter Ks. The Sukhoi Fitter series of ground attack fighters has been continually developed and today the latest variant, the Fitter K, forms the backbone of Warsaw Pact forces in Europe.

# INTRODUCTION

The Su-7 Fitter is a dedicated ground attack fighter designed and built by the Sukhoi Design Bureau (OKB), one of the primary OKBs in the Soviet Union. Over the past thirty years, the Fitter series has emerged as one of the most successful aircraft built in the Soviet Union since the end of the Second World War. Currently, more then half of all tactical ground-attack fighter regiments in the Soviet Union and Warsaw Pact are equipped with one or more Sukhoi Fitter variants.

This impressive aircraft flew for the first time during the mid-1950s, and is considered to be an Eastern contemporary of the North American F-100 Super Sabre. While the Super Sabre has long since been retired, the Sukhoi Su-17 and Su-22, both progressive developments of the basic Su-7 (Fitter A), are the backbone of tactical airpower in the Eastern nations. The Fitter series is a fine example of the Russian method of progressively upgrading a proven aircraft over a long period of time. The Su-22 Fitter J also has the doubtful privilege of being on the losing side in the first air combat involving variable-geometry wing fighters when two Grumman F-14A Tomcats shot down two Libyan flown Fitter Js over the Gulf of Sidra on 19 August 1981.

Pavel Ossipovich Sukhoi, designer of this highly successful series of ground-attack fighters, was born on 10 July 1895 at Glubokoye in Western Byelorussia. After high school, he joined the University of Moscow, and later attended the Moscow School of High Technology where he attended classes given by N.E. Zhukovskiy, the founder of the Central Institute for Aerodynamics and Hydrodynamics (TsAGI). Pavel Sukhoi had shown a vital interest in aircraft ever since his early youth; however, his studies were interrupted by the First World War and in April 1916 he entered the Russian Army. He saw action on the Northwestern Front where he earned the rank of Master Sergeant.

After the war, he returned to the University in 1920 and after graduation joined the TsAGI as a draftsman in 1924. Later, a paper he wrote on a proposed single-seat fighter design impressed Professor Andrej N. Tupolev so much that he offered Pavel Sukhoi a position as an aircraft designer in the Tupolev OKB. While at Tupolev, Sukhoi developed a number of aircraft which carried the Tupolev OKB designations ANT-5, ANT-31, ANT-29, and ANT-25.

In December 1938 Sukhoi left Tupolev and founded his own experimental design bureau. He designed a number of aircraft including the Su-1 (I-330), a high altitude fighter first introduced during 1939, and a short range bomber design, the Su-2, which was built in small numbers (approximately 500 aircraft) before his factory had to be evacuated behind the Ural Mountains after the Germans invaded Russia in the summer of 1941. That same year, Sukhoi designed a dedicated ground-attack aircraft as a competitor to the Ilyushin Il-2 Stormovik. The single seat Su-6 was powered by an ASh-71 engine and had a top speed of 360 mph.

Sukhoi progressively improved the Su-6 and developed a two seat variant of the Su-6 under the designation Su-6III. This aircraft reached the prototype stage during 1944 and was reported to have excellent handling qualities and a performance that was, in many aspects, superior to the Il-10. Because the Ilyushin Il-10 Stormovik was already in service, and changing the production lines over to the Su-6 would cause serious delays, the Su-6 was not adopted and the aircraft never progressed beyond the prototype stage.

## S-22 Prototype

After the end of the Second World War, the Sukhoi Design Bureau built a number of fighter and ground attack prototypes, however, none of these designs reached produc-

**The Sukhoi Su-6III was the first dedicated ground-attack aircraft built by the Sukhoi OKB. Although superior to the Ilyushin Il-10, the aircraft did not progress beyond the prototype stage.**

tion. On 27 November 1949 the Sukhoi Design Bureau was disestablished during a reorganization of the entire Soviet aviation industry. Sukhoi's staff was returned to the Tupolev OKB, and Sukhoi was assigned as Andrej N. Tupolev's deputy. While under the Tupolev OKB, Sukhoi continued to develop new fighter designs and was appointed to head a newly-formed Flight Research Center which closely cooperated with the TsAGI in Moscow.

After Josef Stalin's death in 1953, Sukhoi was allowed to reform his own design bureau. During the nearly four years he had worked under Tupolev, he had been allowed to pursue his own research on a supersonic jet fighter design. Initial design work had begun during 1950 and now that his OKB was reformed, Sukhoi and his staff immediately began work, in December 1953, on the first prototype, designated the S-1 (Strelovidnyi, Sweptback). The S-1 prototype was equipped with a 62 degree swept-back wing and was powered by an AL-7 turbojet engine developing 14,300 pounds thrust.

The AL-7 engine had been developed by the pioneer of the jet engine development in the USSR, Archip Michailovich Lyulka. The Lyulka OKB developed the first experimental jet engine in the Soviet Union, the RD-1 (Reaktiwni Dwigatjel Reaction Engine) during 1934, and had built the first true Soviet jet engine, the TR-1, during 1945. The TR-1 became the forerunner of the TR-7 jet engine which entered production under the designation AL-7 (AL stood for Archip Lyulka). The AL-7 series of engines powered the Il-54, Tu-98, as well Sukhoi's chief competitor for a supersonic fighter production contract, the Mikoyan I-370.

**The S-22 prototype was fitted with seven S-3K air-to-ground rockets on vertical mounts under each of the two wing pylons. The S-22 designation stood for the 22nd experimental fighter prototype built by the Sukhoi OKB. The prototype made its first flight in April of 1957.**

The Sukhoi S-1 prototype emerged as a single-seat tricycle landing gear fighter-bomber, which featured an extremely clean and streamlined area- ruled fuselage. The wing was mid-mounted with a 62 degree sweep. The horizontal tail surfaces were also swept back at the same angle. The vertical stabilizer was moderately swept back and gracefully faired into the fuselage spine. The jet inlet was at the extreme nose and was fitted with a conical centerbody shock cone which was variable, that is, it moved in and out to adjust for the differences in airflow at supersonic speeds. The engine inlet air ducts were split to pass on either side of the single-seat pressurized cockpit and forward retracting nose landing gear, with the engine occupying the rear fuselage. The wide-track, levered-suspension, main gear rotated some 50 degrees to lie flat in the wing ahead of the main wing spar. The S-1 was the first Soviet built fighter to be designed with a variable shock cone and provision for carrying unguided air-to-ground rockets in pods as part of its armament.

On 8 September 1955, the S-1 prototype made its first flight with Soviet test pilot COL Andrej Grigorjevitch Kotshetkov at the controls. COL Kotshetkov was a highly experienced jet test pilot, having been involved with the Soviet Air Force evaluation of captured German Messerschmitt Me 262 jet fighters during August of 1945 and had carried out twelve flights in the Me 262A-la. He had also worked on jet test projects under the Lavochkin OKB, including the La-220B interceptor and La-250 long range interceptor. Kotshetkov, along with other Soviet test pilots, reported that the handling characteristics and performance of the S-1 were impressive, however, they considered the armament to be too light. The S-1 prototype was introduced to the Soviet public at the Aviation Day Air Show at Tushino Airport near Moscow on 24 June 1956.

Alongside the S-1 prototype, Sukhoi also displayed the delta winged Sukhoi T-3 prototype. The T-3 was a direct development of the S-1 using the same basic fuselage, horizontal stabilizers, and vertical stabilizer, mated with a delta wing. The T series of prototypes were intended to fill the interceptor-fighter role and evolved into the highly successful Su-9 (NATO reporting name Fishpot) series of interceptors. Continual development work on the Su-9 led to the Su-11 and ultimately to the Su-15 Flagon, which is still one of the primary interceptor fighters in the Soviet Air Defense Force.

Work with the S-1 prototype continued and the prototype attained a speed of Mach 2 during flight tests held in the summer of 1956. The development program suffered a setback when the prototype S-1 was totally destroyed in a crash on 21 November 1956, killing test pilot I.N. Sokolov. Fortunately, this accident did not seriously delay the test program because the second prototype, designated the S-2, had joined the program during early 1956. Over the course of the test program a number of S-1 prototypes were built to test various aerodynamic improvements and equipment changes. By early 1956, the first prototype equipped with an afterburning AL-7F (F for Forsirovanniy, i.e. boosted) turbojet was delivered, and this aircraft was used to set a new Soviet national speed record of 1,348.41 mph in December of 1957.

During 1957, the Soviet Air Force selected the Mikoyan MiG-21 as its new day fighter and decided that the Sukhoi fighter was best suited to the ground attack role. The Air Force felt that the S-1 would be an ideal aircraft to re-equip the Frontal Aviation (tactical) Regiments of the Soviet Air Force. Sukhoi then worked on modifying the S-1 for the ground attack role. The first prototype, designated the S-22 (S-22 stood for the 22nd fighter prototype built since the Sukhoi OKB was reformed during 1953) flew for the first time in April 1957 and was powered by a 19,840 lbst Lyulka AL-7F-1 turbojet engine. The prototype carried no internal armament but was equipped with four pylons (two under-fuselage and two underwing) to accommodate seven S-3E unguided air-to-ground rockets which were carried on vertical racks below each pylon.

During the development program which was intended to optimize the S-22 for the fighter-bomber role, a number of improvements were incorporated to the prototype. The horizontal stabilizers were changed to all-flying slab stabilizers with anti-flutter balance rods, and the control system was modified with an ARZ-1 artificial feel system for the horizontal stabilizers. Four rear fuselage mounted speed brakes, arranged to form an 'X' when viewed from the front, were installed on the prototype. The nose was modified becoming less tapered, increasing the area of the nose intake allowing a greater airflow for the engine. The centerbody shock cone was modified and now housed an SRD-5 ranging radar. Two spring loaded auxiliary blow-in air inlet doors were added to each side of the nose to increase airflow to the engine under certain low speed conditions. The wing was modified with a redesigned trailing edge which gave the wing a kinked appearance and housed additional flaps. To lower the landing roll out, a drag chute was installed in a housing in the lower fuselage behind the main landing gear wells. With these changes, the prototype began State acceptance trails during January 1958. After successfully completing these trials later that year, the aircraft was ordered into production at Novosibirsk under the designation Sukhoi Su-7.

## Sukhoi Fighter Family Development

**The delta winged Su-9 interceptor (NATO reporting name, Fishpot) used the same basic fuselage and tail as the Su-7B. The Su-9 served with the Home Defense Forces of the Soviet Air Force.**

# Development

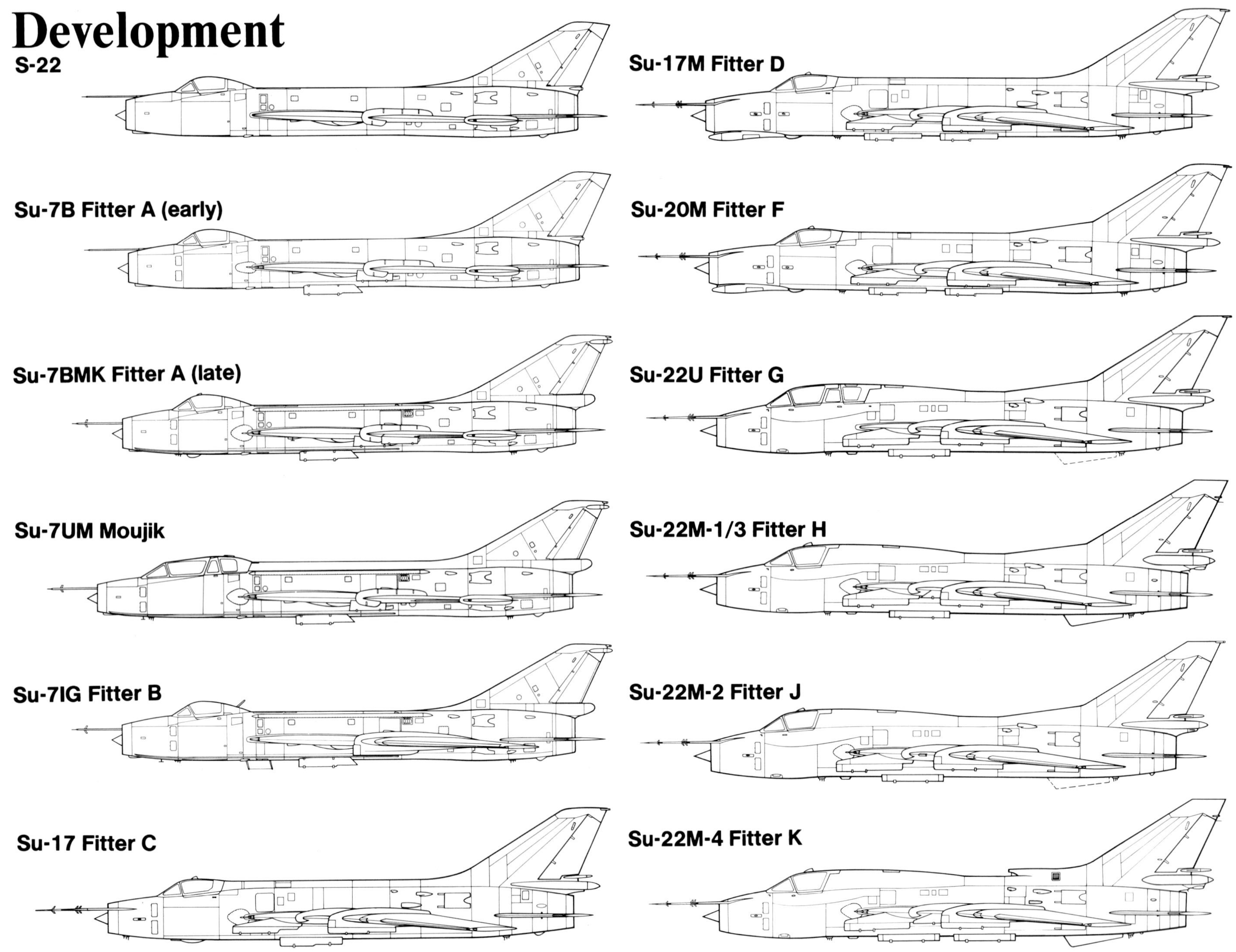

# Su-7 Fitter A

The first production Su-7s were delivered to Soviet Frontal Aviation units during the course of 1958 under the service designation Su-7B (B for Bombardirovshckik, fighter-bomber). Production Su-7Bs (which received the NATO reporting name Fitter A) differed from the prototype S-22 in a number of ways.

The Su-7B was equipped with improved avionics including an SRO-2 IFF set and both VHF and UHF radios. The armament was increased and now included a 30MM Nudelmann-Richter NR-30 cannon installed in each wing root, fed from 70-round ammunition boxes which curved around the fuselage in the space between the fuselage skin and engine air intake ducting. The NR-30 was a well-proven weapon having been first introduced into Soviet service during 1954; it weighed 29.93 pounds, fired at a rate of 900 rounds per minute and had a muzzle velocity of 2559.05 feet-per-second. Firing trials carried out by the U.S. Air Force with captured weapons revealed that the 30MM armor-piercing ammunition fired by the NR-30 can pierce not only the thin armor of a personnel carrier but also the top and rear armor of a main battle tank, such as the American M60. Installation of the cannons in the wing roots made it necessary to install a steel anti-blast panel on each side of the fuselage directly opposite the gun muzzle to protect the fuselage skinning from damage when the guns were fired.

The production Fitter A was cleared to carry a wide range of armament on the two fuselage and two inboard wing pylons. Early Su-7Bs were armed with UB-8 rocket pods containing eight Type S-5 57MM unguided, hollow-charge air-to-ground rockets. The warhead of these rockets had a penetration capability of some 220MM of armor plate. Besides these rockets, the Fitter A could carry various free fall bombs, such as the FAB 100, 250 and 500 kg bombs (220, 551, and 1,102 pounds respectively). The Fitter's internal fuel capacity of 646.7 gallons, carried in both wing and fuselage tanks, proved to be insufficient in service because of the high fuel consumption of the AL-7F-1 engine at the low levels normally flown by fighter-bombers. As a result, the Su-7B normally carries a pair of 158 gallon-drop tanks on the fuselage pylons, reducing usable weapons loads to 2,200 pounds (1,100 pounds on each wing pylon). The high fuel consumption of the AL-7F-1 is typical of early Soviet turbojet engines and seriously affected the Fitter's combat radius. When belly tanks are not carried, range is restricted to about 155 miles, however, this figure is further and dramatically reduced if the engine afterburner is used.

**Red 02, an Su-7B of a Soviet Frontal Aviation unit is armed with a UB-8 rocket pod on each wing pylon. Early Fitter As lacked the fuel/control cable fairings on the fuselage spine which were common on later variants.**

**A Soviet pilot boards his Su-7B Fitter A for a mission. The Su-7B had the air data boom mounted on the nose centerline. The early boom also lacked yaw and pitch sensor vanes.**

Despite its shortcomings in range and armament, the Sukhoi Su-7 has proven to be a reliable and very stable gun platform at low levels even under turbulent conditions. The sharply swept wing gives good supersonic performance and the generous flap area and wide track landing gear gives the Fitter good airfield performance and the ability to operate from rough unprepared strips. One drawback of the sharply swept wing design, however, was a loss of lift due to aerodynamic span-wise airflow. This problem was corrected on the production Su-7B by the installation of two large airflow fences on each wing, one just outboard of the wing pylon and the other at the wing tip.

After a relatively small number of Su-7Bs had left the production line at Novosibirsk, an improved model, the Su-7BM (modified fighter-bomber) was placed into production. The Su-7BM featured a fuel line/cable duct fairing on each side of the fuselage spine running from the main avionics bay area to the rear fuselage just forward of the vertical stabilizer. The air data instrument boom was moved from its position on the center top of the nose cone to the upper right side of the nose cone. The air data boom itself was also improved with the addition of both yaw and pitch sensor vanes.

Both the Su-7B and Su-7BM are equipped with a Type KKO-2 cockpit climactic system which both pressurizes and heats the cockpit (no air conditioning is provided). The Type KS-4 ejection seat can be used at all altitudes above 330 feet and at speeds up to 680 mph. The Su-7BM had further avionics upgrades including an ARK-5 radio compass, a MRP-48P radio beacon receiver, a RV-2 radio altimeter, and a Type ASP-3VM radar ranging gunsight.

The armament was upgraded by replacing the UB-8 eight-shot rocket pod with the UB-16 pod holding sixteen 57MM rockets. This pod became the most commonly used armament on the Su-7BM. After service introduction with Soviet Frontal Aviation units, including the Group of Soviet Forces in East Germany (GSFG), the Su-7BM was cleared for export, with examples going to India, Czechoslovakia, Poland, and Egypt.

The Su-7BM has been progressively improved with new avionics and other equipment. Indian Air Force Su-7BMs were modified with a revised drag chute housing at the base of the vertical stabilizer holding two ribbon style drag chutes instead of the single drag chute housing mounted under the fuselage of Soviet Su-7BMs. Additionally, these export Fitter As were also configured with an additional weapons pylon mounted on the wing outboard of the wing fence. Most of the Fitter As in service were retrofitted with a rear-view mirror mounted on the forward portion of the movable canopy. These features were later introduced on the production line and became standard on the Su-7BMK. During the mid-1980s a number of Su-7BMs remained in service with both the Indian and Czechoslovakian Air Forces, after a service life of nearly thirty years.

Efforts to shorten the landing run of the Su-7BM led to the design of an improved landing gear. This new landing gear was installed on the third production variant of the Fitter A, the Su-7BKL (KL, Koleso-Lyzhanyi, wheel/ski). The Su-7BKL was numerical the most important variant of the Fitter A series. The new landing gear featured strengthened oleo legs, an enlarged nose wheel, low pressure tires, and bulged nose gear doors. For use on unprepared fields, a steel skid was mounted on the main landing gear legs, outboard of the main wheels. These skids were retractable and were kept in the retracted position if the Fitter was operated from a hard-surfaced runway. For operations from grass or unprepared strips, the skids could be extended on landing, dramatically increasing the Fitter's braking capabilities. The skids could also be used to assist braking on snow or ice covered fields. This modified landing gear allowed the Su-7BKL to be operated from much smaller advanced unprepared fields. The use of such fields was a vital part of overall Soviet planning should war ever erupt in Europe.

In addition to the skids, the Su-7BKL was modified with the same drag chute housing first introduced on the Indian Air Force Su-7BMs. The drag chute housing was moved from under the fuselage to the base of the vertical stabilizer and enlarged to house two ribbon drag chutes instead of the single parachute used of the Soviet Su-7BM. The enlarged drag chute housing did reduce the area of the rudder slightly, although this

The Su-7BM had fuel line/control cable fairings on the fuselage spine and yaw/pitch vanes on the air data boom, which was offset on the starboard side of the nose. This Czech Air Force Su-7BM, Black 5320, has been fitted with an Olive Drab canvas cover over the cockpit to protect the canopy while the aircraft is parked.

reportedly has had no effect on aircraft handling. The new drag chutes reduced the landing roll of the Su-7BKL to approximately 2,250 feet.

For short takeoffs, or to assist with heavy loads under hot and high conditions, the Su-7BKL can be fitted with two Type SPRD-110 rocket assist takeoff (RATO) rockets which are carried on either side of the rear fuselage, just below the wing trailing edge. These RATO units give the Su-7BKL an additional 6,600 pounds of thrust for takeoff. The RATO rockets are ignited automatically once the aircraft reaches a preset airspeed, however, there is provision for manual firing by the pilot should the automatic controls fail. The SPRD-110 rockets were first demonstrated on a Sukhoi Su-7BKL at the Domodedovo Airshow in July 1967. The demonstration Fitter A, coded Red 26, was specially configured for the demonstration and had the wing and fuselage pylons and wing root cannons removed.

The Su-7BKL incorporated further avionics improvements including an improved gunsight and a Sirena 2 tail warning system. The antenna for the Sirena 2 was mounted on the top of the rudder just below the tip of the vertical tail. The Su-7BKL also had the anti-blast panels on the fuselage sides opposite the cannon muzzles enlarged.

This Su-7BM Fitter A, Black 5323, of the Czech Air Force carries a Red star marking above the Czech national insignia on the vertical stabilizer. The air intake cover, normally fitted to Su-7s whenever the aircraft is parked, is in Red.

## Air Data Boom

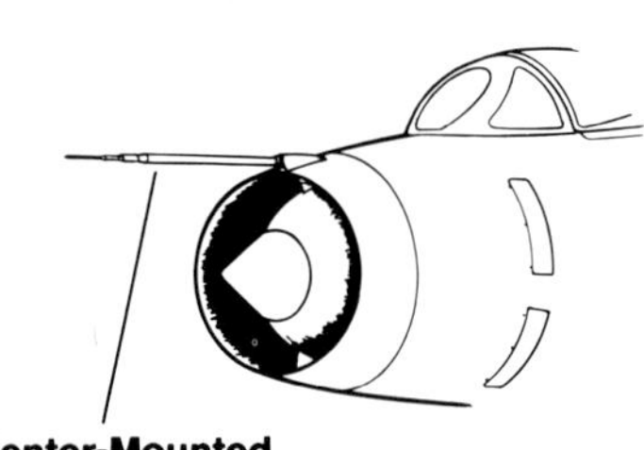


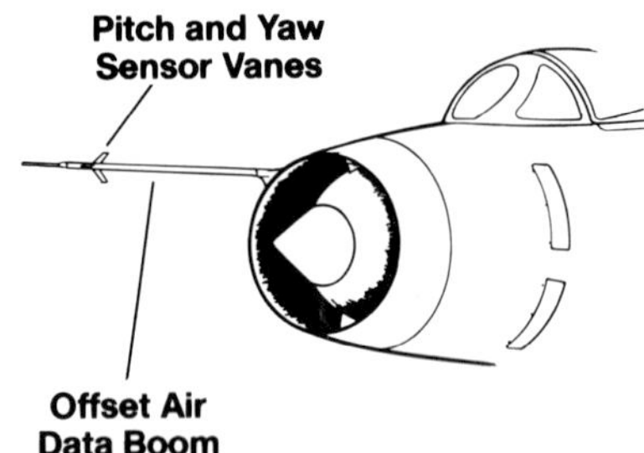

This Su-7BM Fitter A, Black 5024 of the Czech Air Force carries a special marking on the port side of the nose to honor a Communist Brigade. Such markings are seldom seen on Warsaw Pact aircraft.

A Czech Air Force pilot boards his Fitter A, Black 5323, in preparation for another mission. His helmet bag is hanging on the boarding ladder and will be handed to him by a ground crewman. The aircraft is configured with 158 gallon drop tanks on the under-fuselage pylons to increase the limited endurance of the Fitter A.

   In Soviet service, Su-7BMs and Su-7BKLs were often operated in the same Frontal Aviation Regiments and both were progressively upgraded with new equipment. All late production Su-7BKLs were retrofitted with a rear view mirror and two additional outer wing weapons pylons making them virtually indistinguishable from the last production variant, the Su-7BMK. The Su-7BKL has also been widely exported and serves in the air forces of Afghanistan, Cuba, Czechoslovakia, Egypt, India, Poland, Syria, and Vietnam (contrary to published reports, the German Democratic Republic and Hungary never operated Su-7s). Su-7BMs and Su-7BKLs saw combat in the 1968 India-Pakistani War and Su-7BKLs were used by the Egyptian Air Force in several of the Arab/Israeli Wars. Both the Indian and Egyptian pilots praised the Fitter's handling qualities and speed at low level, however, both air forces reported that the Fitter was vulnerable to small caliber anti-aircraft fire, especially to hits in the engine bay.

**Late in their service career with the Czech Air Force, surviving Fitter As were painted in a camouflage paint scheme and were modified with rear view mirrors on the canopy. Black 5017 is one of the remaining Su-7BMs still in service with the Czech Air Force, based at Hradec Kralove Air Base.**

   The Su-7BMK became the last production variant of the Fitter A series. This variant incorporated two additional two wing weapons pylons, as well as the canopy-mounted rear-view mirror as standard production items. The Su-7BMK also featured further improvements to the avionics and a number of late-production aircraft were equipped with an improved Sirena 3 tail warning radar receiver. The Su-7BMK also was fitted with a KM-1 zero-zero rocket ejection seat replacing the earlier Type SK ejection seat. The KM-1 seat boosts the pilot to an altitude of 150 feet in the event of a ground level ejection. The seat also incorporated an improved Type NAZ-7 emergency survival kit housed in the seat headrest.

   A number of Su-7BKL and Su-7BMK Fitter As in service with the Egyptian Air Force have reportedly been retrofitted with advanced Western electronics replacing the installed Soviet equipment, however, details of these modifications are currently unavailable.

**An Su-7BM Fitter A, Black 5027, of the Czech Air Force taxies out for takeoff, while a pair of Su-7BMs climb out on their mission. At the height of their service in the Czech Air Force, the 10th Tactical Division operated at least forty-two Fitter As.**

A formation of three Soviet Air Force Su-7BKLs shortly after takeoff. Each aircraft is armed with UB-16 sixteen shot 57MM rocket pods on the wing pylons and 158 gallon drop tanks on the fuselage pylons.

The Su-7BKL featured a bulged nose wheel door and enlarged gun blast shields on the fuselage sides. This Soviet Air Force Su-7BKL Fitter A taxies out for another mission past a line of MiG-21 Fishbed and MiG-17 Fresco fighters.

This Su-7BM Fitter A of No 222 Squadron (Killers), Indian Air Force has been updated with an additional wing pylon on each wing immediately outboard of the main landing gear, a drag chute housing at the base of the rudder, and a Sirena 2 radar warning system antenna at the top of the rudder.

## Su-7 Fitter A Series

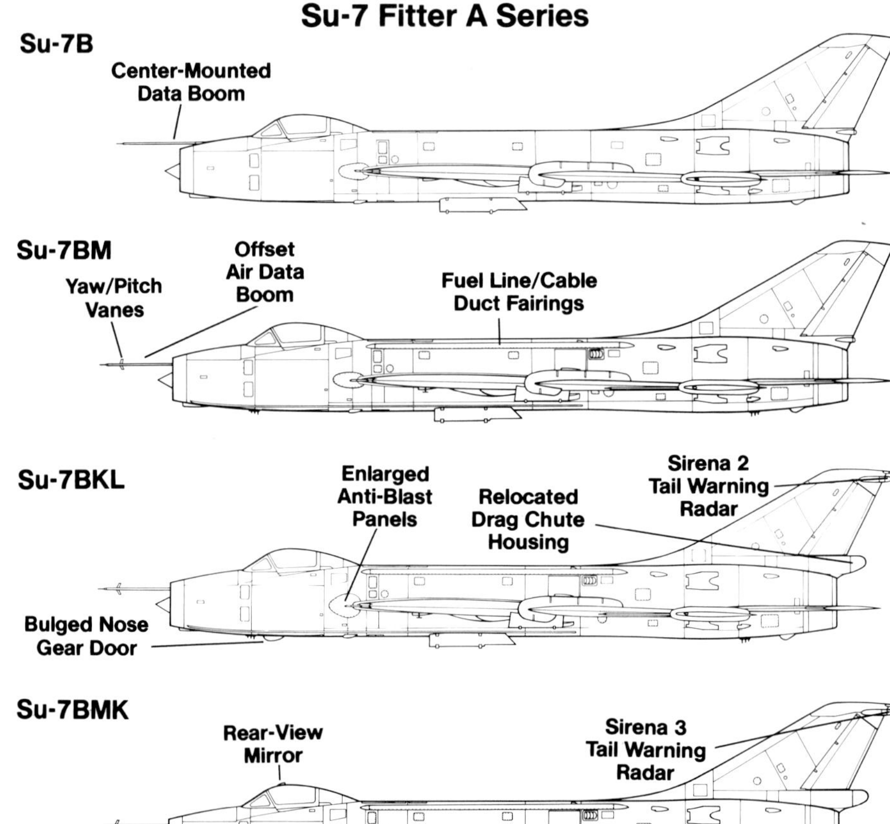

A mixed formation of Polish Air Force Fitter As. Red 818 is an Su-7BMK while Red 15 is an Su-7BKL. The use of different variants of the Fitter A within the same regiment is not uncommon among Soviet and Warsaw Pact fighter regiments.

## Fuselage Development

**Su-7B**

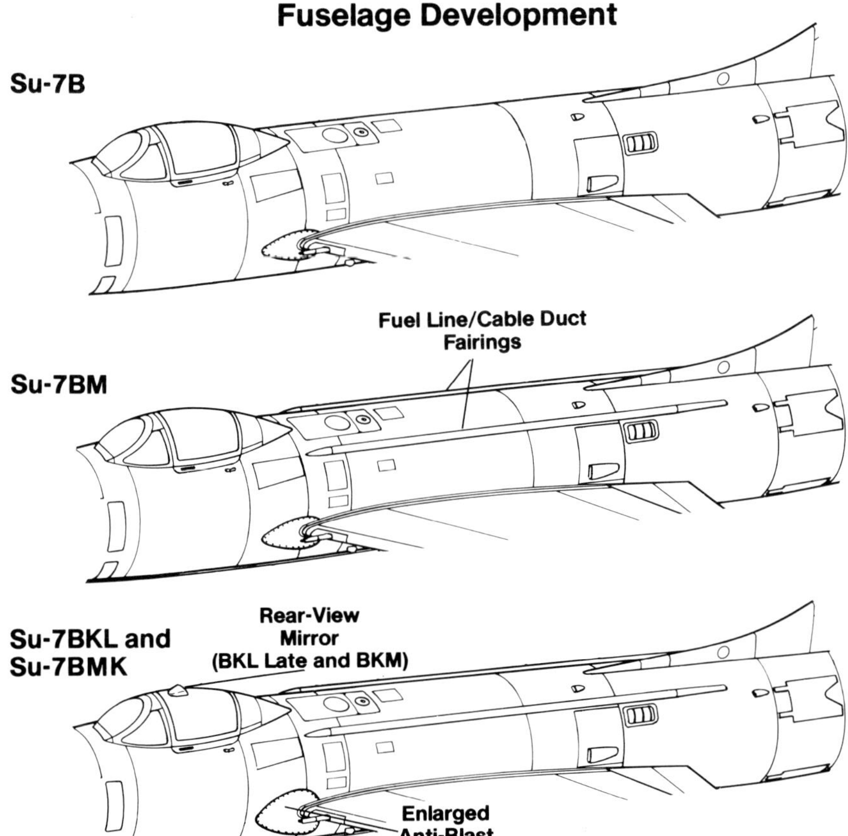

**Su-7BM**

Fuel Line/Cable Duct Fairings

**Su-7BKL and Su-7BMK**

Rear-View Mirror (BKL Late and BKM)

Enlarged Anti-Blast Panel

Ground crews conduct maintenance on a Polish Air Force Su-7BKL Fitter A, Red 20. The aircraft tactical number (20) is repeated on the air intake cover in White. The dark areas in front of the wing root cannon are blast marks from the NR-30 cannon. The tow bar, attached to the nosewheel is also connected to each main landing gear mount by a wire cable.

Black 6514, an Su-7BMK of the Czech Air Force taxies out during a Warsaw Pact exercise. The camouflage netting in the background is large enough to accomodate a Fitter A and provides the fighter with excellent camouflage when parked on unprepared grass fields.

11

# Specifications

## Sukhoi Su-7BKL Fitter A (Early)

| | |
|---|---|
| **Wingspan** | 29 feet 3½ inches |
| **Length** | 57 feet |
| **Height** | 15 feet |
| **Empty Weight** | 18,360 pounds |
| **Maximum Weight** | 29,600 pounds |
| **Powerplant** | One 14,198 lbst Lyulka AL-7F turbojet |
| **Armament** | Two NR-30 30мм cannons and 2,200 pounds of ordnance |
| **Performance** | |
|   **Maximum Speed** | 1,085 mph 36,000 feet |
|   **Service ceiling** | 49,210 feet |
|   **Range** | 120-285 miles (loaded) 900 miles (four drop tanks) |
| **Crew** | One |

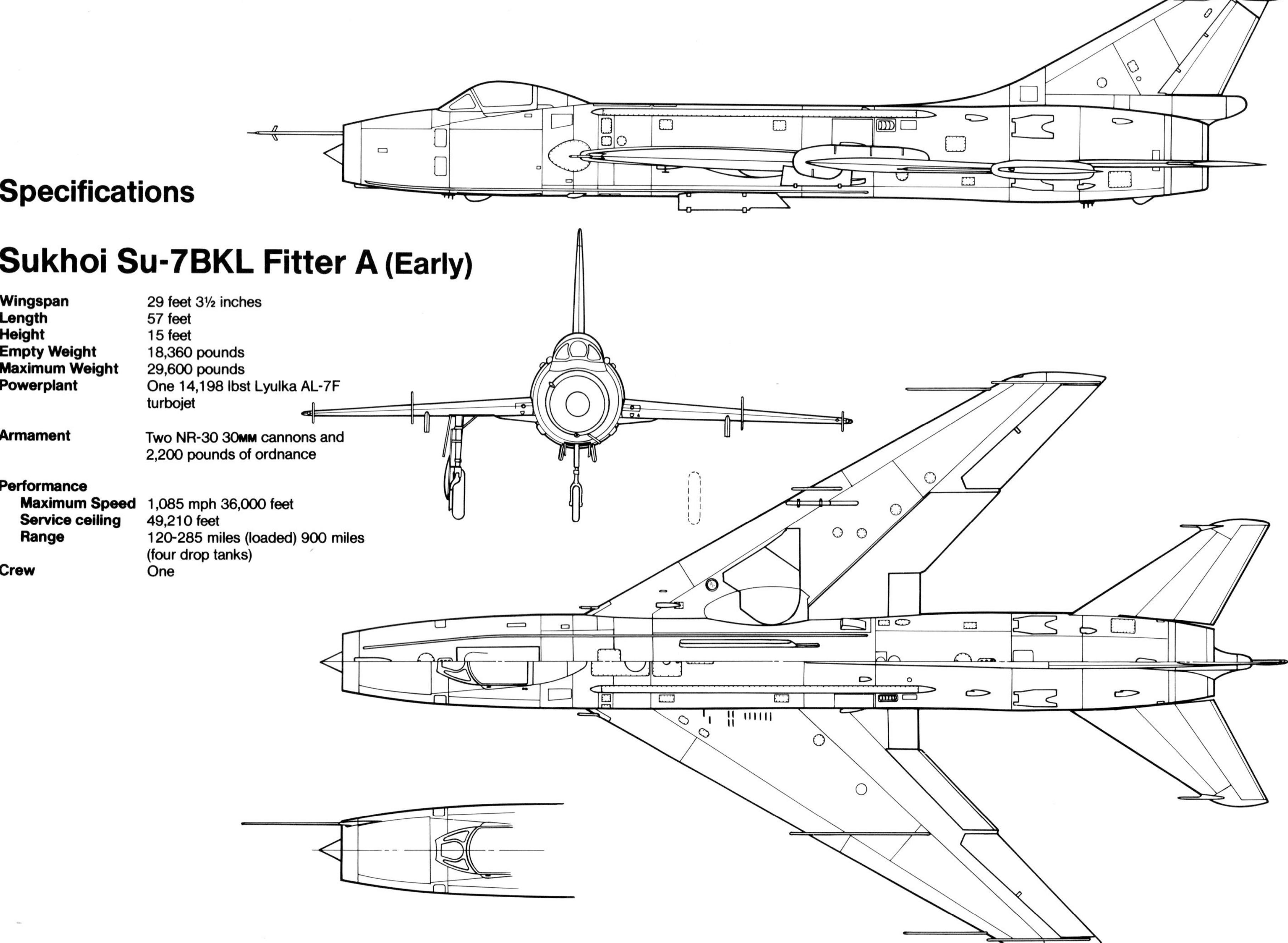

A pair of camouflaged Algerian Air Force Su-7BMKs take off on another mission. Both aircraft are in a clean configuration, carrying no external fuel tanks, indicating that the mission is probably a short duration flight.

Four Polish Air Force Su-7BMKs share the flight line with an Su-7UM Moujik trainer (Red 70), an Su-7BM (Red 09), and a MiG-15UTI Midget trainer (foreground). The support vehicle in the background is a Tatra 138 fuel truck.

## Tail Development

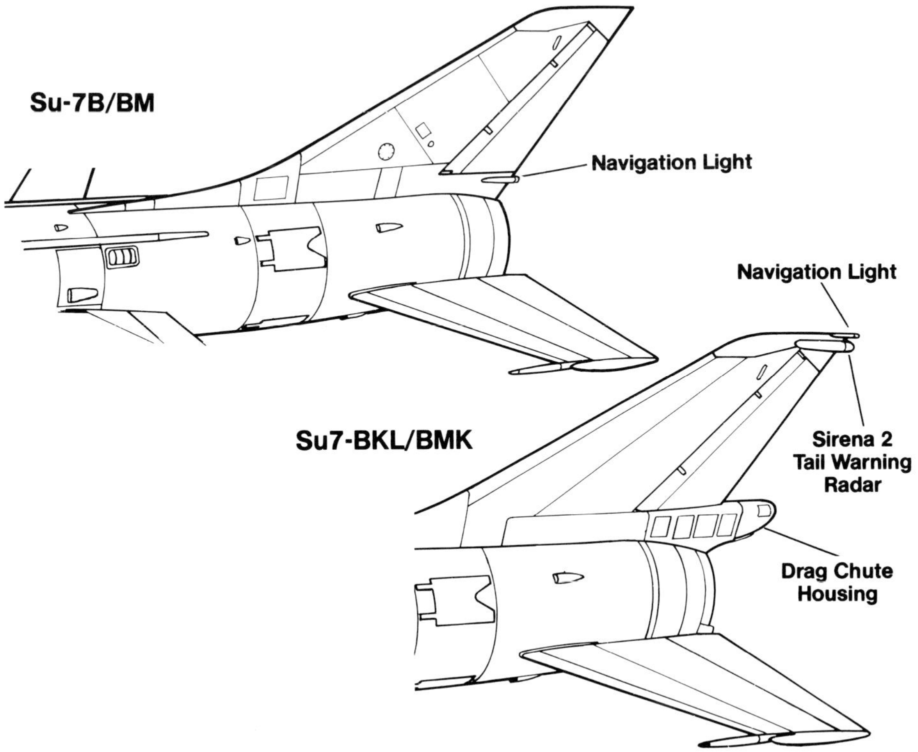

This ground crewman is placing a repacked drag chute in the drag chute housing on a Fitter A. Both the Su-7BKL and Su-7BMK use two such drag chutes, both housed in the same streamlined fairing at the base of the rudder.

A Polish Air Force Su-7BMK Fitter A lands on a wet runway with the aid of its twin drag chutes. The weather in Eastern Europe often makes the use of drag chutes a necessity because of wet or icy runways.

An Su-7BMK Fitter A of the Czech Air Force climbs out on another mission. The braking skids on the main landing gear are visible just in front of the main landing gear strut. The Czech Air Force operated a limited number of Su-7BMKs.

## Landing Gear Development

### Su-7B/BM

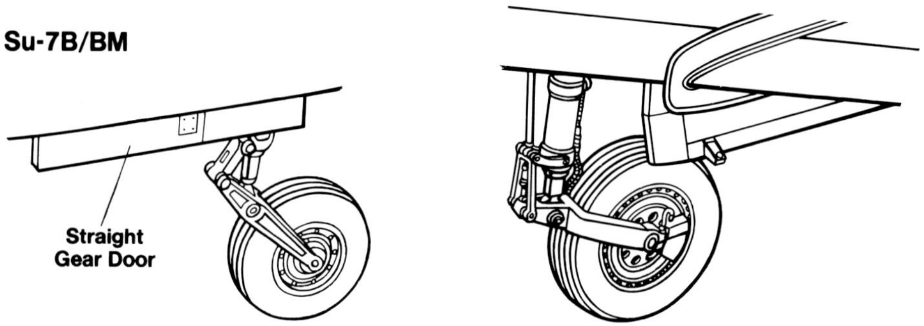

### Su-7BKL/BMK

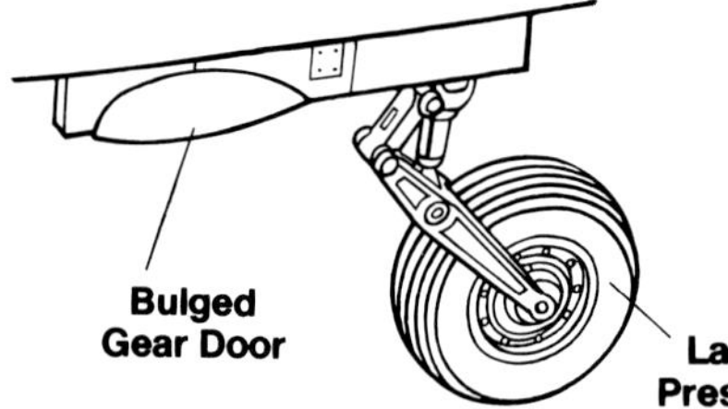


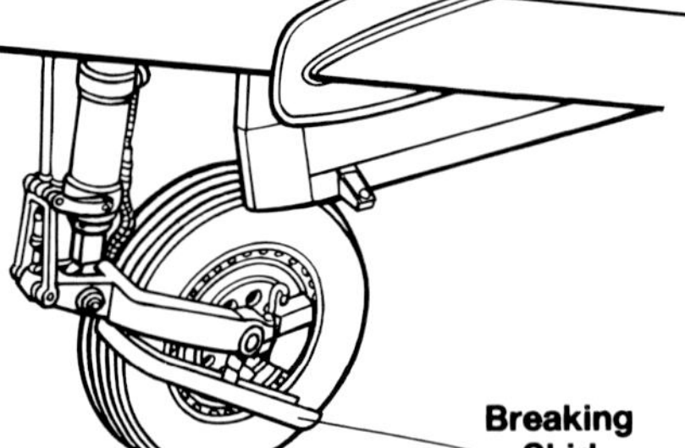

A Polish ground crewman reloads S-5 57mm rockets into a UB-16 rocket pod on the outer wing pylon of a Fitter A. When the pod has been reloaded, the end cap will be replaced and the arming wires will be plugged into the pylon electrical system.

## Weapons Pylons

### Su-7BM/BKL

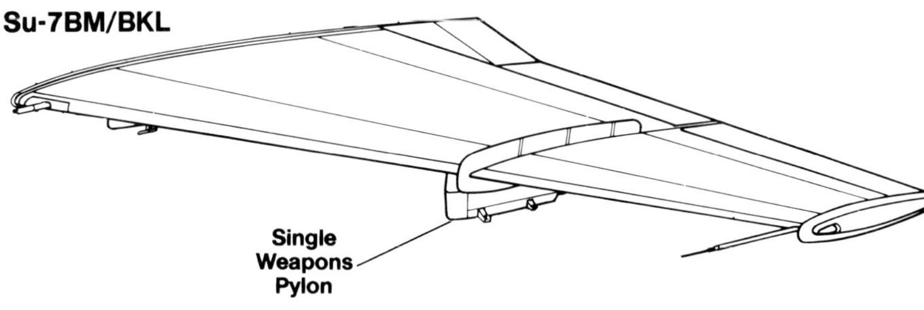


### Su-7BMK

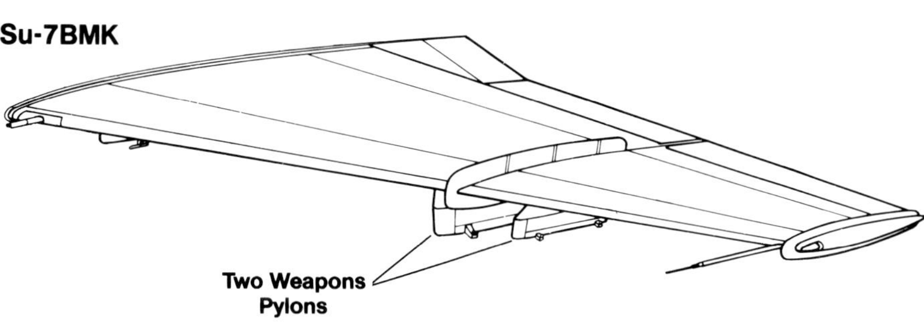

A Polish Air Force pilot in the cockpit of an Su-7BMK Fitter A. The Black oxygen hose on the pilots helmet connects directly into the aircraft's oxygen system. The flight suit is a fully pressurized suit normally used for high altitude-flight.

A Polish ground crew refuels an Su-7BMK Fitter A. The small dark circle on the fuselage side is the open refueling port. The rocket pods in the foreground and on the wing pylon are UB-16 pods each containing sixteen Type S-5 air-to-ground rockets.

# Su-7U Moujik

Usually when the Soviets introduce a new single seat fighter into production, the OKB responsible for the aircraft will also develop, in parallel, a two-seat trainer variant to allow service pilots to easily transition from older aircraft to the new fighter. The Su-7 was no exception. Sukhoi developed a two-seat trainer variant of the Fitter by lengthening the nose of an Su-7BM airframe one foot and replacing the fuselage fuel tank with a second cockpit for an instructor pilot. The trainer prototype retained the full armament of the single-seat Su-7 and after a short testing period entered production under the designation Su-7U (NATO reporting name Moujik).

The production Su-7U Moujik retains two NR-30 wing-root cannons, two underwing pylons and two fuselage pylons to allow it to be used for weapons training or, if need be, actual combat. To accommodate the second cockpit for the instructor, the nose was stretched one foot in front of the cockpit and a second cockpit was installed in the space between air inlet ducts formerly occupied by the fuselage main fuel tank. The front canopy was also enlarged to improve visibility for the student pilot.

While the canopy on the single seat Su-7 is a rearward sliding canopy, the two-seat Su-7U has canopies that are hinged at the rear and open upwards. The rear cockpit canopy is blended into the fuselage with a pronounced a dorsal spine, which was required to maintain the aerodynamics of the fuselage. Forward visibility from the rear cockpit, especially in the landing configuration, is blocked by the student's seat, and to overcome this problem, a retractable mirror/periscope viewing system has been fitted to the top of the instructor's canopy. The periscope can be deployed at speeds below 375 mph. The Su-7U is equipped with two Type SK ejection seats and has an electronics suite that is basically similar to the single seat fighter.

**Red 54, a Soviet Air Force Su-7U Moujik carries the 'Excellent Aircraft' award on the nose in Red. This award is painted on Soviet aircraft when the maintenance crews have reached and maintained certain strict requirements. The 'T' shaped antenna in front of the nose wheel door is a radio altimeter antenna.**

**Soviet instructors and students on the flight line of a Soviet Air Force base walk past a pair of Su-7U Moujik trainers. The Su-7U features an upward opening canopy while the single-seat Su-7 Fitter A has a rearward sliding canopy.**

The Moujik featured several small changes from the Su-7BM Fitter A; the T shaped radio altimeter antenna was repositioned from under the port wing-root to the underside of the nose forward of the nose wheel doors, and the instructor's cockpit has a simulation control panel which feeds simulated emergency situations/conditions to the student's instrument panel.

## Canopy Development

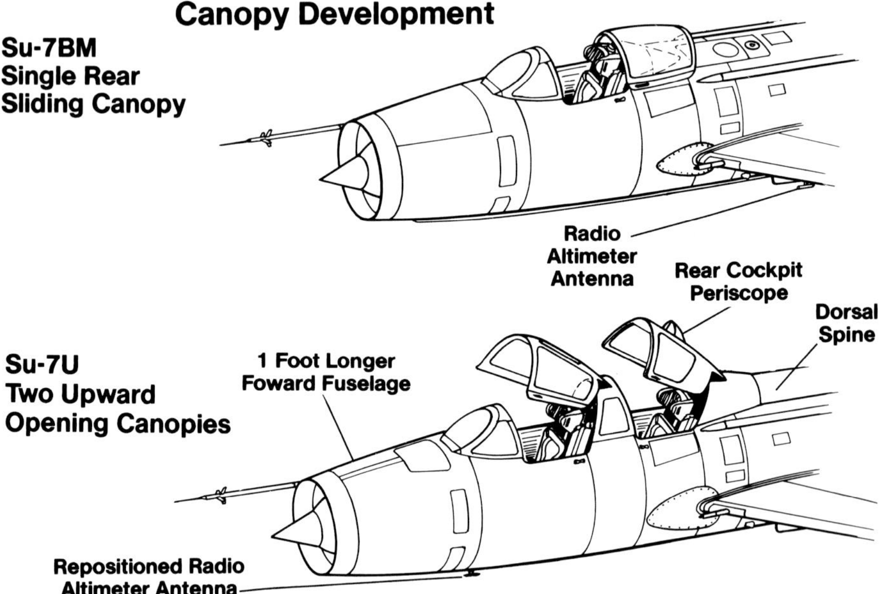

# Su-7UM Moujik

The Su-7UM was the second generation Su-7U trainer to enter production and was basically an upgraded variant based on the single-seat Su-7BMK airframe. The Su-7UM was built in larger numbers than any other two seat Su-7U variant and was progressively upgraded throughout its production life. Based on the Su-7BMK airframe, the Su-7UM features the same twin drag-chute housing at the base of the rudder and Sirena 2 tail warning radar as the single seat fighter. Late production Su-7UMs were also upgraded with KM-1 Zero-Zero rocket assisted ejection seats.

Most training missions conducted with the Su-7U/UM are carried out with two 158 gallon drop tanks on the fuselage pylons, while the wing pylons may be used to carry a variety of weapons including UB-16 rocket pods and FAB 100/250 kg bombs, for the weapons training role. Most Warsaw Pact pilots convert to the single-seat Su-7 Fitter A after completing an advanced training course in the Aero L-29 or L-39 trainer, then transition, at the squadron level, to the Su-7U/UM. After gaining sufficient experience with the handling qualities of the Su-7U/UM, the student then progresses to the single seat Su-7.

The Su-7U/UM has been widely exported and serves in the air forces of Algeria, Egypt, India, Libya and most Warsaw Pact nations. A number of these aircraft are still operational in India, Egypt, Czechoslovakia, and Poland.

There have been numerous references to the designations Su-7UKL and Su-7UMK; however, it is believed that these designations are in error. The designation Su-7UKM would indicate a Moujik equipped with the skid landing gear of the Su-7BMK, and there is no evidence that any Su-7U series aircraft was ever equipped with this type of landing gear.

**A Soviet instructor demonstrates one of the maneuvers to be performed on this flight with the aid of a model Fitter. The aircraft tactical number, 86, in Red with a Black outline on the nose, is repeated on the drop tanks in Black.**

Red 706 is a well-worn Su-7UM Moujik of the Polish Air Force. The forward canopy on the Moujik is larger than that of the single seat Su-7 Fitter A, giving the student pilot a better all around view from the cockpit. The Moujik is a combat-capable trainer carrying the same armament as the Fitter A.

A Polish Air Force Su-7UM deploys its twin drag chutes to reduce its landing roll. The poor forward vision from the intructor's cockpit is somewhat offset by use of a retractable periscope/mirror viewing system, which is always extended on takeoff and landing.

A Czech Air Force Su-7UM, Black 0509, takes off on a training sortie. The instructor's periscope/mirror is fully extended to provide the instructor with a degree of forward view over the nose. The circular object in front of the nose wheel is a retractable landing light.

A Polish Su-7UM taxies past a row of jet blast deflectors after returning from a mission. The jet blast deflectors are metal troughs designed to funnel the exhaust of parked aircraft up and away from the ramp.

A ground crew refuels a Su-7UM Moujik of the Polish Air Force in front of a camouflaged, hardened aircraft shelter. These shelters are designed to house a single aircraft and are hardened to protect the aircraft from all but a direct bomb hit. The truck is a Czech Tatra 138.

# S-22I/Su-7IG

During the early 1960s, both Mikoyan-Guryevich (MiG) and Sukhoi, the two leading design bureaus in the Soviet Union concerned with fighter and fighter-bomber development, carried out research on variable geometry winged aircraft. Both OKBs were supported in their research efforts by the Central Institute for Aerodynamics and Hydrodynamics (TsAGI) in Moscow; however, these efforts were very limited during the first half of the decade, both as a result of a basic lack of available research data and by the fact that the concept was not seriously accepted by higher authorities within the Soviet Union.

MiG and Sukhoi each approached the problem from different viewpoints. The Mikoyan-Guryevich team developed the Ye-23I (which evolved into the MiG-23 Flogger), a fighter prototype with full variable geometry wings similar to the type used on the American General Dynamics F-111, while the Sukhoi design team, under the leadership of Nikolai Zyrin, decided to modify a basic Su-7 with varible geometry outer wing panels. The varible geometry Fitter project was given the Sukhoi experimental designation S-22I (I for Izmenyaemaya/Variable).

The S-22I was a less radical approach than that undertaken by MiG, incorporating variable geometry to the outer wing panels and retaining the basic 62 degree swept wing for the inner panels which remained fixed to accommodate underwing ordnance pylons and the wing root NR-30 cannon. The problem of location of the wing pivot point was solved by using the outboard external wing hard point, which was of fairly heavy construction and was, additionally, a part of the wing load bearing structure. The incorporation of the wing pivot bearing at this point was virtually trouble free, particularly since the aerodynamic loads at this point on the wing were only a fraction of those encountered at the wing root.

The choice of a half-span variable geometry wing rather that a full span variable geometry wing was also dictated by Soviet Air Force requirements. The main thrust of the modification was to improve the takeoff and landing performance of the Fitter, rather than any requirement for increased loiter times, or longer range. One of the main drawbacks of the earlier Su-7 Fitter A series was its need for a long, hard-surfaced runway whenever operating with full loads. The landing speed of the Fitter A was also excessively high and had resulted in a high accident rate among Warsaw Pact air forces. The use of the variable geometry half-span wing, along with the addition of leading edge slats would reduce the landing speed by approximately 62 mph and allow for a shorter takeoff run with a full load. Additionally, it was estimated that the variable geometry

The SU-7IG on final approach for landing with the varible geometry wing at full forward sweep and the wing leading edge slots in the fully extended position. The demonstrator carried no armament and was basically an Su-7BM airframe modified to test the new wing configuration.

The Su-7IG Fitter B technology demonstrator during its first public demonstration at Domodedovo Air Base in July of 1967. The aircraft was given the NATO reporting name Fitter B and was thought to be a one of a kind experimental aircraft. It was actually a technology demonstrator, test bed, and prototype for a new Fitter series.

winged Fitter would be able to carry twice the ordnance load some 30 per cent further.

The S-22I (also known as the Su-7IG Izmenyaemaya Geometriya/Variable Geometry) first flew on 2 August 1966 and was demonstrated at Domodedovo on 9 July 1967 as part of the Soviet Aviation Day airshow. The demonstrator was an Su-7BM fuselage modified with a twin drag chute housing at the base of the rudder (similar to the Su-7BKL) and variable geometry outer wing panels. Powered by the proven 15,432 pound thrust AL-7F-1 engine, the Su-7IG was unarmed and carried test equipment antennas on the fuselage near the rear of the canopy and on the underside of the fuselage behind the nose wheel doors.

When the aircraft was first revealed, it was given the NATO reporting name Fitter B and was incorrectly evaluated as a one-of-a kind technology demonstrator rather than a true prototype of a new Fitter series. In reality, the S-22I/Su-7IG served not only as a technology demonstrator, but also as a prototype, providing the Soviets with the basic data needed to begin construction of a variable geometry variant of the Fitter.

## Wing Development

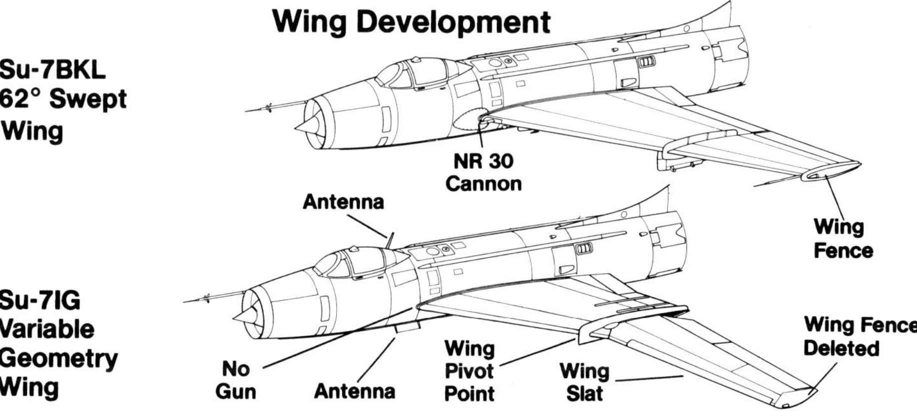

# Su-17/20 Fitter C

Based on engineering data obtained in testing the Su-7IG, the Soviets produced a small number of pre-production variable geometry wing Sukhoi ground-attack aircraft during 1970 under the designation Su-17. These aircraft were assigned to Frontal Aviation units for operationally testing. These early Su-17s had an identical wing sweep system to that used on the Su-7IG. The wing sweep was manually controlled and had three positions; full forward (28 degree wing sweep), full back (62 degree sweep), and one intermediate position.

These Su-17s differed from the Su-7IG in having an additional smaller wing air flow fence mounted inboard of the large wing fence which now mounted a weapons pylon. The aft sliding canopy was changed to a rear-hinged clamshell style canopy that was faired into the fuselage with a pronounced fuselage dorsal spine. An additional weapons pylon was added to the wings, being mounted at the wing root just forward of the landing gear wheel well. A second sensor boom was mounted on the nose on the port side incorporating sensors for the fire control system's computers. The Sirena 3 radar warning receiver was also relocated, now being mounted at a slightly different angle on top of the rudder just below the tip of the vertical stabilizer.

The nose wheel was identical to that of the earlier Su-7BMK; however, the nose wheel doors were changed from a single bulged door to a two-piece nose wheel door with the bulged portion normally being closed when the aircraft is on the ground. The main wheel skids of the Su-7BKL and BMK were deleted on the Su-17 and the main wheel doors were redesigned. Field trials with the Su-7BKL Fitter A had showed that the skids were not as helpful as hoped, and, by deleting them, the weight of the main landing gear structure was reduced.

The avionics package on the Su-17 included a R5B-70 HF radio which had its antenna mounted in a blister on the fuselage dorsal spine just behind the cockpit.

Service trials were conducted with two squadrons of pre-production Su-17s which proved highly successful and convinced Soviet Air Force officials that the variable geometry Su-17 was far superior to the conventional wing Su-7 series. The aircraft was ordered into series production with the first production Su-17s entering service with the Soviet Air Force Frontal Aviation units during 1971.

Production Su-17s differed from the pre-production aircraft in a number of ways. To increase performance and ordnance loads, production Su-17s were fitted with a more powerful 24,000 pound thrust Lyulka AL-21-F3 engine in place of the 15,432 pound thrust AL-7F-1 engine. The internal fuel capacity was unchanged (1,200 gallons), however, the aircraft could now carry up to four 211 gallon drop tanks.

**This pre-production Su-17 was used to test various components intended for use on the production swing wing Fitter under service conditions. The aircraft featured a new upward opening canopy, dorsal spine (similar to the Su-7U Moujik), and repositioned Sirena 3 radar warning system antenna.**

An early production Su-17 Fitter C of a Soviet Frontal Aviation unit on final approach to an East German air base. Production Su-17s featured an additional sensor boom fitted on the starboard side of the nose and the Sirena 3 antenna moved to the base of the rudder.

## Wing/Fuselage Development

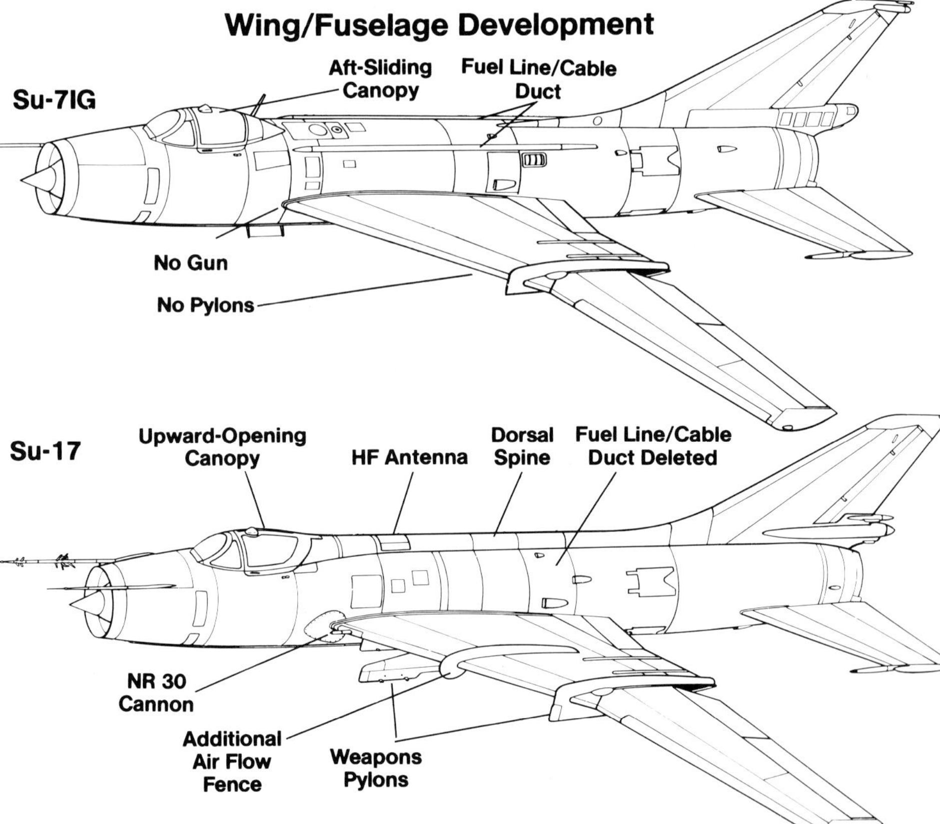

The armament options for the Su-17 were similar to those used on the Fitter A; however, the Fitter C can carry a total of 7,000 pounds of ordnance, some 3,000 pounds more that a Fitter A. The Su-17 is cleared to carry a mix of bombs (including nuclear weapons), gun pods, rockets pods, and guided missiles (AA-2 Atoll or AA-8 Aphid air-to-air missiles and AS-7 Kerry air-to-surface missiles) on four under-wing pylons and two under-fuselage pylons.

The Su-17 can also be used as a tactical reconnaissance aircraft, carrying a large multi-sensor reconnaissance pod under the fuselage. The front half of the pod contains the cameras and other sensors, while the rear portion of the pod is a fuel tank. When the reconnaissance pod is fitted, the two under-fuselage pylons are deleted and replaced by a large single pylon on the centerline from which the pod is suspended.

A number of improvements dictated by service use have been introduced on the Su-17 during its production cycle. The nose has been slightly stretched and an angle-of-attack transmitter vane has been installed on a blister on the port side of the nose just behind the intake. The fuel line/cable fairing ducts on either side of the dorsal spine, a typical feature on the Fitter A and the pre-production Su-17s, were deleted. The Sirena 3 radar warning radar receiver has been repositioned from the top of the rudder to the base of the rudder just above the drag chute housing, which now contains a single braking parachute and has been reduced in size with a more pointed cover.

The three ram air inlets on the rear fuselage, used to cool the engine bay liner, were repositioned on the Su-17 being higher on the fuselage sides. A number of early Su-17s were fitted with four fuselage pylons arranged in pairs, however, most Fitter Cs have the standard two fuselage pylons, including those exported outside Russia.

Avionics upgrades included installation of a SRD-5M ranging radar, a SRO-2M Odd Rods IFF, a Sirena 3 tail warning radar, and an ASP-5ND optical gunsight. Other avionics installed in the Fitter C include an ARK-10 radio compass, an RV-UM radio altimeter, a MRP-56P radio beacon receiver, SOD-57m ATC/SIF, a Type NI-50BM Doppler Radar Computer, a Type SP-50 ILS, and a RSBN-2S short range navigational receiver. The radio equipment includes R5B-70 HF and RSIU-5 UHF radios, an ARL-S Data Link transceiver, and an R-831 UHF radio.

**Red 7125 of the Polish Air Force is a late production Su-20 Fitter C. The Su-20 was the export designation for the Su-17 Fitter C. Reportedly, Polish Air Force Fitter Cs were identical to Soviet Air Force first-line Su-17s.**

**A Polish Air Force pilot climbs into his Fitter C, Red 03, at a Polish Air Force base. The aircraft is armed with a pair of UB-16 rocket pods. The fairing , midway down the port side of the nose, is the mounting for the angle-of-attack sensor vane.**

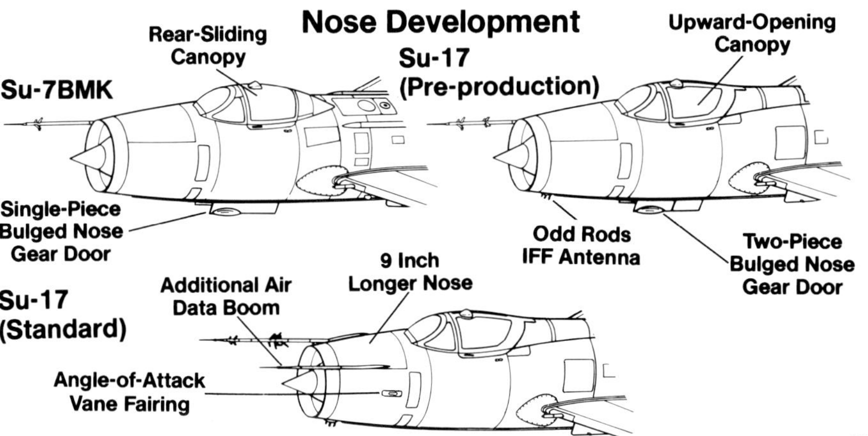

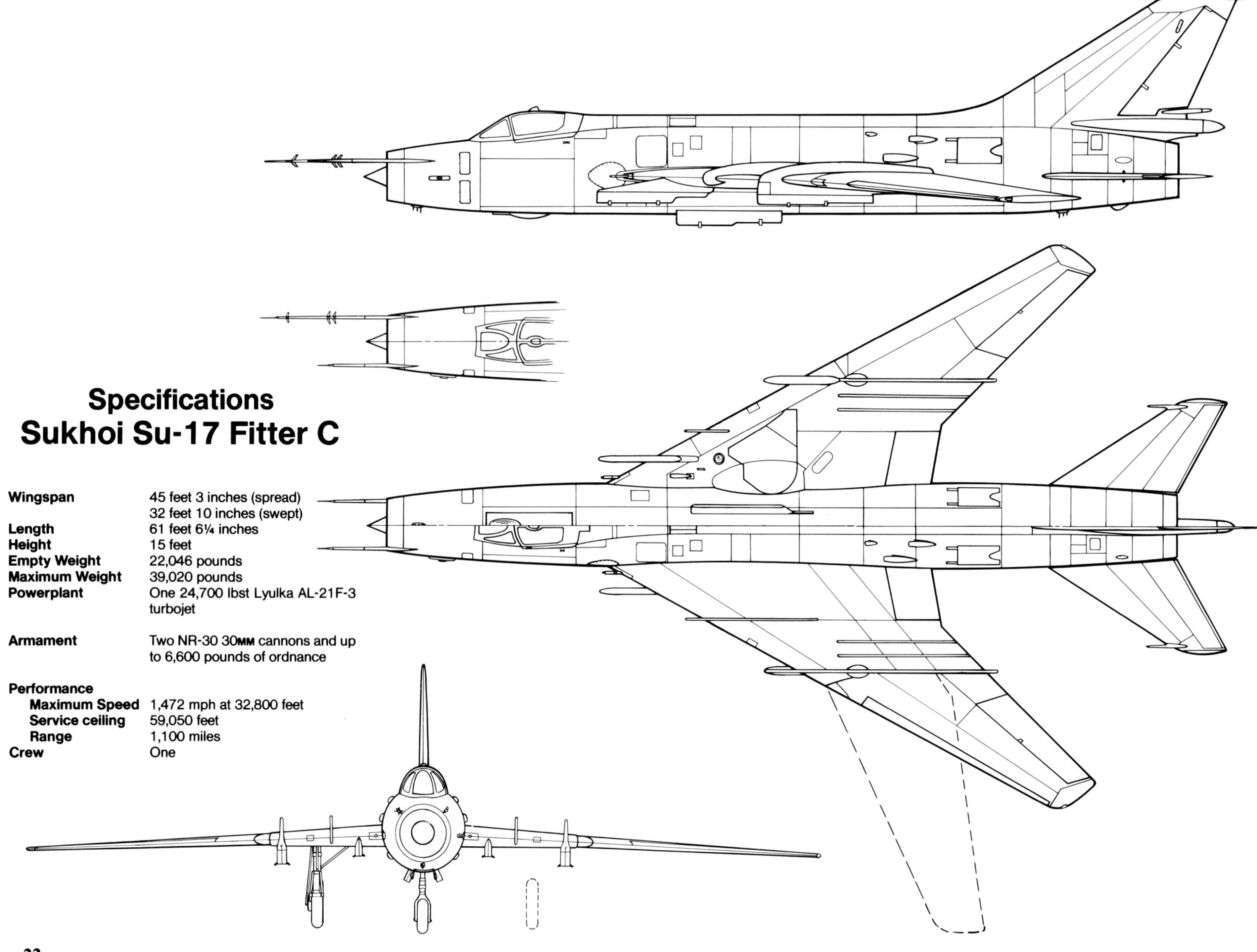

# Specifications
# Sukhoi Su-17 Fitter C

| | |
|---|---|
| **Wingspan** | 45 feet 3 inches (spread) |
| | 32 feet 10 inches (swept) |
| **Length** | 61 feet 6¼ inches |
| **Height** | 15 feet |
| **Empty Weight** | 22,046 pounds |
| **Maximum Weight** | 39,020 pounds |
| **Powerplant** | One 24,700 lbst Lyulka AL-21F-3 turbojet |
| **Armament** | Two NR-30 30мм cannons and up to 6,600 pounds of ordnance |
| **Performance** | |
| **Maximum Speed** | 1,472 mph at 32,800 feet |
| **Service ceiling** | 59,050 feet |
| **Range** | 1,100 miles |
| **Crew** | One |

The Su-17 entered service with the Soviet Air Force and immediately began to replace Su-7s in first line Frontal Aviation regiments. Three regiments of Su-17s were deployed as part of the Group of Soviet Forces Germany (GSFG) being based at Allstedt, Templin, and Neuruppin. The deployment to Germany brought the new Sukhoi to the attention of NATO, and the aircraft was allocated the NATO reporting name, Fitter C.

During the early Summer of 1974 the first export Fitter Cs were delivered to the Polish Air Force. These aircraft were reportedly designated Su-20 and this designation became common for all export models of the Fitter C. The Polish Air Force thus far is the only Warsaw Pact air force to operate the Su-20 and these aircraft are reportedly identical to first-line Soviet Su-17s. The Polish Su-20s were unveiled for the first time on 22 July 1974 during the celebrations marking the 30th Anniversary of the Socialist Polish Air Force. At least thirty-six Su-20s are known to be in service, based at Pila, as part of the Polish tactical air forces. In case of war, these aircraft would operate alongside some 400 Soviet Fitter Cs based in various countries in Eastern Europe.

Syria became the first country outside the Warsaw Pact to be equipped with the Fitter C. Although externally identical to Soviet Su-17s, these export Su-20s have a somewhat degraded electronics suite. The Syrian aircraft received their baptism of fire during the 1973 Arab-Israeli War. Other air forces that received the Su-20 were Angola, Afghanistan, Algeria, Egypt, Iraq, North Korea, and Vietnam. Reportedly the unit price of a Su-20 delivered to the Middle East during 1975 was quoted at 2 million US dollars, approximately 200,000 dollars more expensive then the earlier Su-7 Fitter As sold to foreign customers.

A ground crew loads an Su-20 Fitter C with an FAB 100 bomb. Three other FAB 100s are on the bomb dolly along with four S-5 57MM unguided hollow charge rockets (normally carried in pods) and belts of 30MM ammunition for the Fitter's NR-30 cannon.

A ground crew loads an FAB 100 bomb on the fuselage pylon of a Fitter C. The Type RK-54 weapons pylon is widely used on various Warsaw Pact aircraft and helicopters including the MiG-23 and Mi-8 Hip. The pylon itself has provision for up to eight mounting bolts; however, only four are used to mount the pylon to the Fitter C.

**Armorers load belted 30MM ammunition into the ammunition bay of a Su-20 Fitter C. The NR-30 cannon carried in each wing root fires a large round which is extremely effective against lightly armored vehicles and can also penetrate the top armor of main battle tanks.**

This Su-20 is equipped 158 gallon fuel tanks on the outboard wing pylons and air-to-air missile rails on the inboard wing pylons. These rails can accomodate either the K-13A (AA-2 Atoll) or K-60 (AA-8 Aphid) air-to-air missile giving the Fitter C a secondary role of air defense.

An Su-20 deploys its drag chute shortly after touch down at a Polish Air Force base. Because of its lower landing speed (62 mph less than a Fitter A), the Fitter C requires only one drag chute instead of the twin chutes used on the earlier Su-7 Fitter A.

Red 4242 an Su-20 Fitter C of the Polish Air Force rolls out with its flaps fully extended. The drag chute will be released after the Fitter C comes to a halt and will be retrieved by the ground crew.

## Tail Development

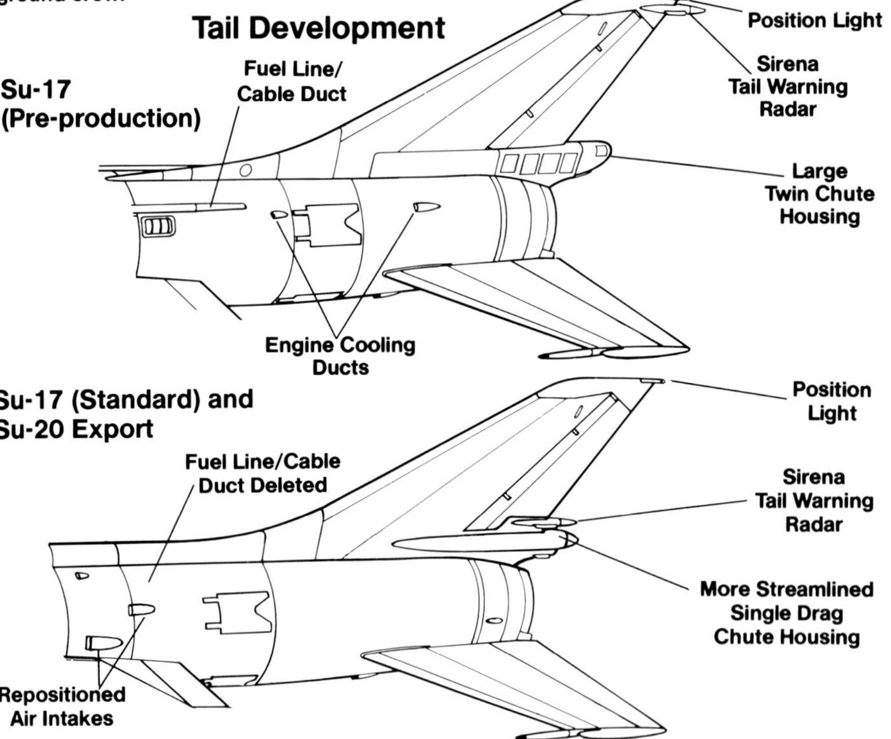

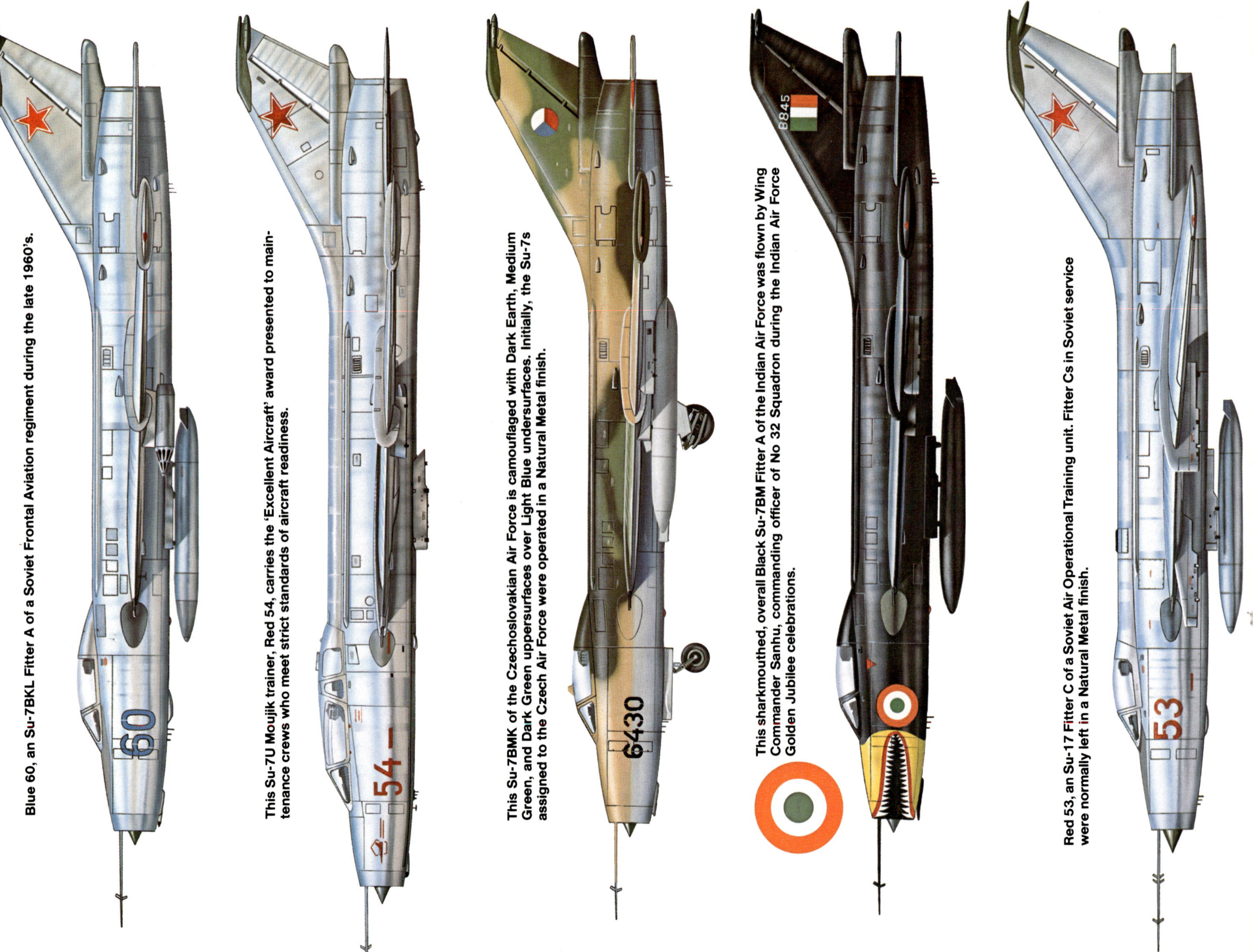

Blue 60, an Su-7BKL Fitter A of a Soviet Frontal Aviation regiment during the late 1960's.

This Su-7U Moujik trainer, Red 54, carries the 'Excellent Aircraft' award presented to maintenance crews who meet strict standards of aircraft readiness.

This Su-7BMK of the Czechoslovakian Air Force is camouflaged with Dark Earth, Medium Green, and Dark Green uppersurfaces over Light Blue undersurfaces. Initially, the Su-7s assigned to the Czech Air Force were operated in a Natural Metal finish.

This sharkmouthed, overall Black Su-7BM Fitter A of the Indian Air Force was flown by Wing Commander Sanhu, commanding officer of No 32 Squadron during the Indian Air Force Golden Jubilee celebrations.

Red 53, an Su-17 Fitter C of a Soviet Air Operational Training unit. Fitter Cs in Soviet service were normally left in a Natural Metal finish.

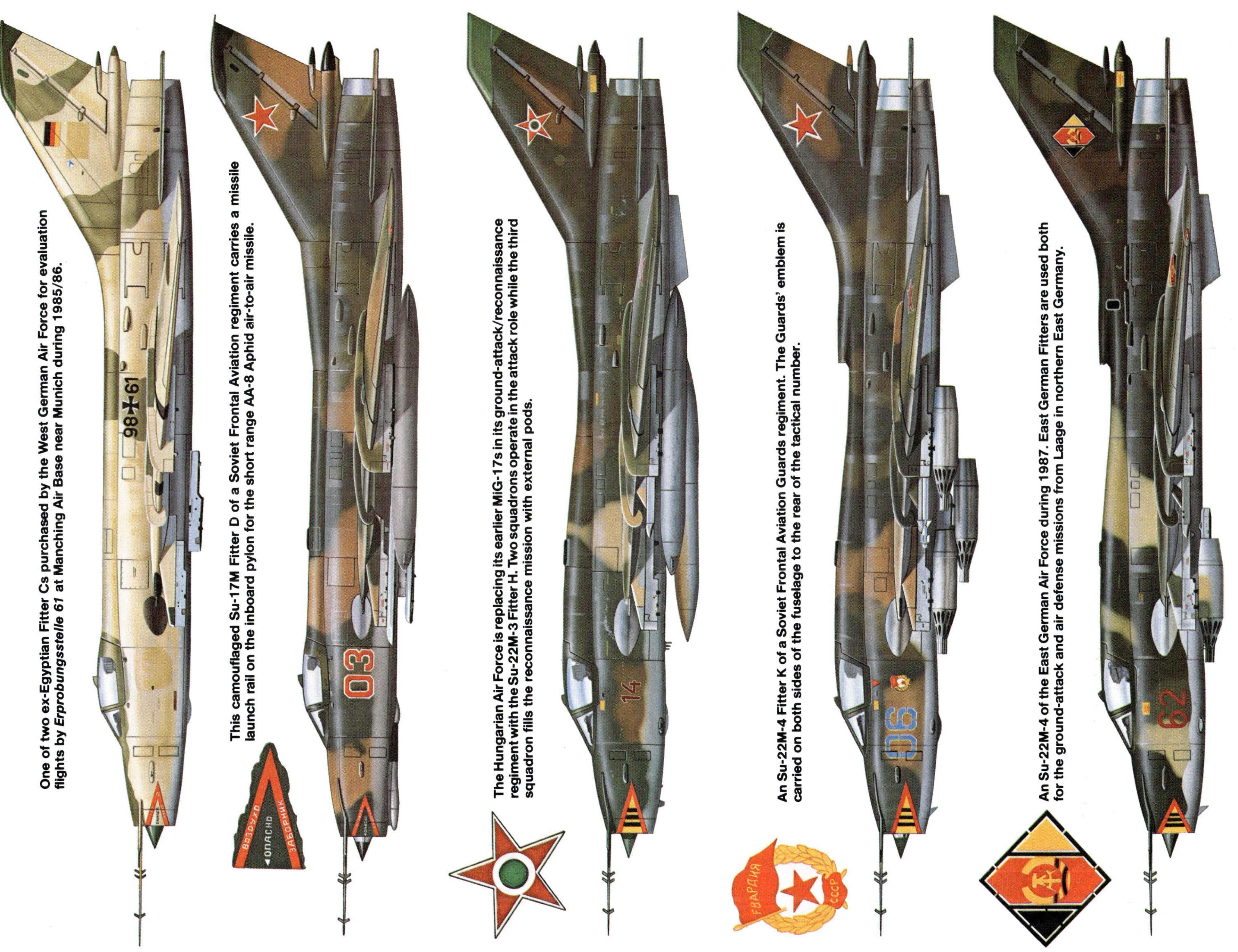

One of two ex-Egyptian Fitter Cs purchased by the West German Air Force for evaluation flights by *Erprobungsstelle 61* at Manching Air Base near Munich during 1985/86.

This camouflaged Su-17M Fitter D of a Soviet Frontal Aviation regiment carries a missile launch rail on the inboard pylon for the short range AA-8 Aphid air-to-air missile.

The Hungarian Air Force is replacing its earlier MiG-17s in its ground-attack/reconnaissance regiment with the Su-22M-3 Fitter H. Two squadrons operate in the attack role while the third squadron fills the reconnaissance mission with external pods.

An Su-22M-4 Fitter K of a Soviet Frontal Aviation Guards regiment. The Guards' emblem is carried on both sides of the fuselage to the rear of the tactical number.

An Su-22M-4 of the East German Air Force during 1987. East German Fitters are used both for the ground-attack and air defense missions from Laage in northern East Germany.

This Su-17 of the Group of Soviet Forces Germany on final approach for landing at an East German airfield has two Black exercise stripes painted on each outer wing panel and is configured with four under fuselage weapons pylons.

This Polish Air Force Su-20 Fitter C carries a UB-16 rocket pod on each inboard wing pylon and a GSh-23L twin 23mm cannon pod on the starboard fuselage pylon. The pod contains a twin barreled 23mm revolver cannon that is highly effective for both air-to-ground and air-to-air use.

A formation of four Polish Air Force Fitter Cs over the Polish countryside. The aircraft are probably conducting a cross country navigation flight and are cruising at a reduced airspeed with the wing in the full forward position to increase their range.

Red 6250, a Polish Air Force Su-20 lands after completing a mission. The rear portion of the nose wheel door is extended; however, the bulged forward portion is retracted. This door opens only during the extension/retraction cycle of the nose wheel and is normally closed.

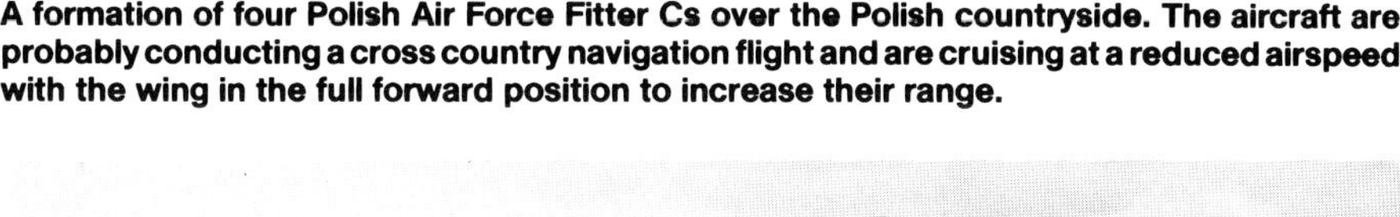

A ground crewman prepares to direct the pilot of this Su-17 Fitter C out of its parking spot. The aircraft is armed with four FAB 100 kg bombs (220 pounds) carried on the inboard wing pylons and fuselage pylons. The small square on the canopy center rail is the viewing port for the rear view mirror.

Su-20 Fitter Cs on the ramp of a Polish Air Force base. The second and third aircraft in line are being refuelled, while a tow bar is positioned in front of the second Su-20. The air intake warning triangle on the nose of all of the aircraft is in Russian, not Polish.

Red 6259, an Su-20 Fitter C of the Polish Air Force takes off with a tactical reconnaissance pod on the fuselage centerline. The pod is twenty-one feet long and contains cameras and electronic intelligence antennas. When the pod is carried, the two under fuselage weapons pylons are replaced by a single centerline pylon.

## Tactical Reconnaissance Pod

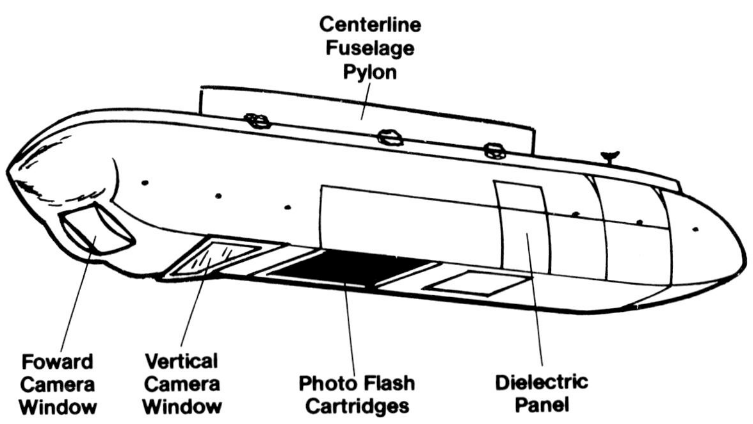

# Su-17M Fitter D and Su-22 Fitter F

During 1976, the Soviets introduced into service an improved variant of the Su-17 under the designation Su-17M. The new variant had the nose section extended forward 15 inches ahead of the cockpit and had a large external chin fairing under the nose ahead of the nose landing gear well. The under nose fairing housed a Doppler terrain avoidance radar antenna and other avionics designed to enhance the Fitter's capability for very low altitude attacks. With the Doppler radar, the Su-17M could fly missions at near ground level, avoiding detection from enemy radar and lessening its exposure to enemy ground fire. To accommodate the Doppler fairing, the Odd Rods IFF antenna under the nose was repositioned from in front of the nose wheel doors to a new position to the rear of the nose wheel doors.

The Su-17M could also carry four fuselage weapons pylons arranged in pairs on the lower fuselage; however, the normal configuration remained two fuselage pylons. To increase the accuracy of weapons delivery, a laser rangefinder was installed in the lower portion of the air intake center-body shock cone. This new Fitter variant was issued to Soviet Frontal Aviation units as a dedicated attack aircraft and received the NATO reporting name Fitter D. The Fitter D was built in limited numbers and was never exported outside of the Soviet Union. Befitting their role as low-level attack aircraft, most of the Fitter Ds were delivered from the factory in a camouflage paint scheme, sharply contrasting with the earlier Fitter Cs, which where all delivered in natural metal.

The Soviets developed an export model of the Su-17M which was fitted with downgraded electronics and other changes depending on the customer. The first Su-17Ms exported were given the NATO reporting name Fitter F and were delivered to the Libyan Arab Republic Air Force. The second export customer was the *Fuerza Aerea del Peruana* (Peruvian Air Force), which took delivery of thirty-six aircraft between 1976 and 1978 followed by an additional sixteen aircraft in 1980. The Fitter Fs delivered to Peru were given the export designation Su-22 and were powered by a Tumansky R-29B engine in place of the Lyulka engine. These aircraft were further modified with a smaller chin fairing under the nose and a raked extension of the vertical fin to offset the deeper nose. The installation of the 27,500 pound thrust Tumansky R-29B engine (the same engine used on the MiG-23 Flogger) resulted in an slightly recontoured rear fuselage and engine exhaust area.

**Red 46, an Su-17M Fitter D of a Soviet Frontal Aviation unit has a large fairing under the nose to accomodate a Doppler radar antenna. To make room for the Doppler fairing the Odd Rods IFF antenna was repositioned from in front of the nose wheel well to a position just behind the nose wheel well.**

**Su-22 Fitter Fs of Escuadron de Caza 11, Los Tigres, (11th Fighter Squadron, Tigers), *Fureza Aerea del Peru* (Peruvian Air Force) at their home base of Limatambo, Peru. The Peruvian Air Force is the only South American air force to operate the Fitter and took delivery of fifty-two aircraft between 1976 and 1980.**

Production of the Su-17 series phased out during 1977 after production of some 800 aircraft. The Fitter D remains in service in the Soviet Union and Poland, and the Fitter F remains in service in Peru were it is expected to remain operational well into the early 1990s. The Fitter C and Fitter D/F have proven themselves to be very reliable aircraft and have one of the lowest accident rates of all aircraft types flown by Warsaw Pact forces.

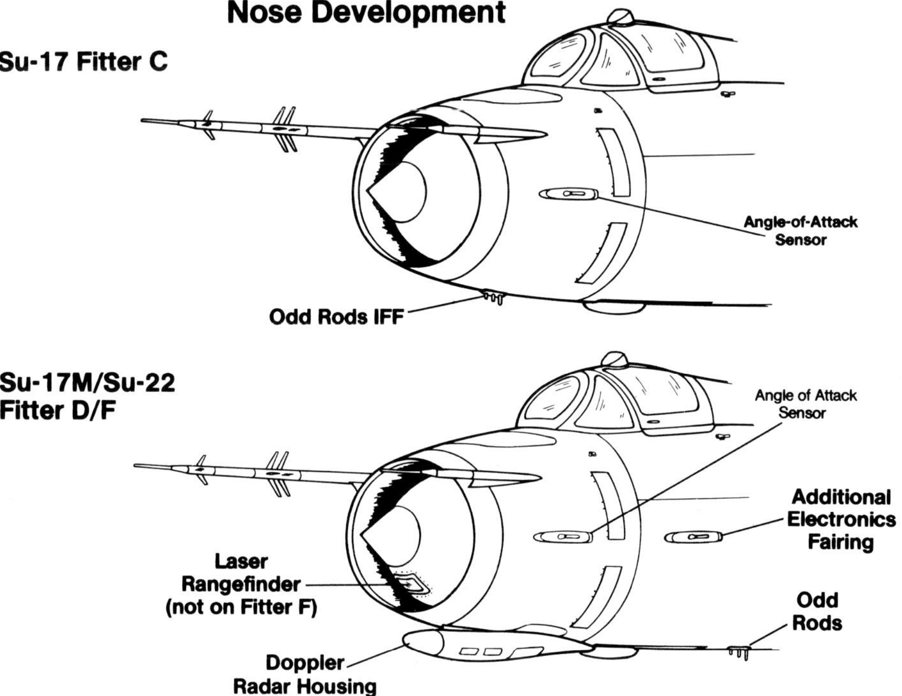

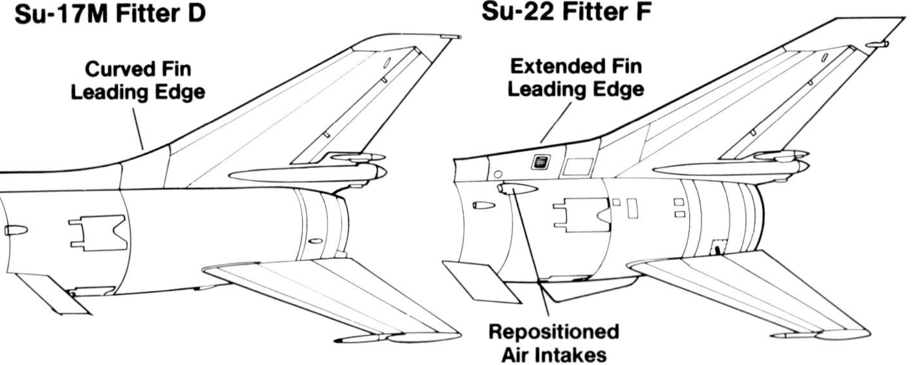

(Above) An Su-22 Fitter F of the Libyan Arab Air Force over the Mediterranean Sea. Libyan Fitters are used to fly surveillance missions over the Gulf of Sidra and have seen combat in Chad supporting Chadian rebels. Several have been reportedly lost to ground fire in Chad.

(Below Left) These Soviet Frontal Aviation crews have just returned from a mission in their Su-17M Fitter Ds. While most Fitter Cs in Soviet service were uncamouflaged, almost all of the Su-17Ms were camouflaged. Red 03 is equipped with missile rails on the inboard wing pylon which can carry either a K-13A or K-60 air-to-air missile.

## Fin Extension

# *Bundesluftwaffe* Fitter C

During 1985, the *Bundesluftwaffe* (West German Air Force) added a most unusual aircraft to its inventory; a Soviet-built Sukhoi Su-20 Fitter C. Two of these aircraft were purchased from Egypt with the intention of conducting a series of both static and flight evaluations of the Fitter C to obtain information on its design, construction, performance, and handling characteristics. German aviation officials, both military and civil, felt that such information was of particular interest in light of the Tornado re-equipment program that was in progress within NATO. The variable geometry wing Panavia Tornado was now the standard fighter-bomber in Germany, England, and Italy. The opportunity to compare a first line Soviet variable geometry fighter bomber with the Tornado was felt to be well worth the costs of the two Fitter Cs.

The two Fitter Cs were dismantled and crated in Egypt before shipment to West Germany. One aircraft was reassembled by aircraft specialists of the *Erprobungsstelle* 61 at Manching Air Field, near Munich Bavaria, while the second aircraft was to be used for spare parts. The original Egyptian markings were overpainted, as was the tactical number on nose. West German national insignia and the fuselage code 98+61 was added, however, the original Egyptian camouflage paint scheme was left intact.

After a close technical examination of the Fitter C and its systems was completed, the first ground tests were begun in late autumn 1985. These were followed shortly by a series of flight trials. Several flight tests were carried out to gather specific information on the performance and handling characteristics of the Fitter C. This was of particular interest to the military in order to develop tactics to be used against the Sukhoi, since NATO is faced by approximately 4,370 Warsaw Pact tactical aircraft, a considerable number of which are late-model Fitters.

The Fitter C retained its armament, however, gun firing and weapon trials were never carried out with the aircraft. The existence of the two Sukhois in West Germany was kept a closely guarded secret until late 1985, when Fitter 98+61 was photographed by a West German reporter and the pictures appeared in several magazines. Apart from the confirmation from the West German Department of Defense that the two aircraft came from Egypt, very little information was officially released, despite a flood of questions from the press.

The evaluation flights continued until the summer 1986 and by that time a total of twenty-five hours had been flown in 98+61. The West Germans received the Su-20 Fitter Cs during the same time frame that the *Luftstreitkrafte* (German Democratic Republic Air Force) received their first Su-22M-4 Fitter Ks.

**The West German Su-20 Fitter C on an evaluation flight over Bavaria. The West Germans were able to closely study the Fitter and as a result they were able to develop tactics to be used against Warsaw Pact Fitters in case of war in Europe.**

**The *Bundesluftwaffe* Su-20 Fitter C on a test flight with the wings in the full forward position. West Germany obtained two Fitter Cs from Egypt and this aircraft was delivered with the lower portion of the outboard wing pylons removed.**

**The *Bundesluftwaffe* Fitter parked on the ramp at Manching Air Force Base. The darker areas on the nose and vertical tail are where the Egyptian Air Force insignia and tactical numbers were painted out.**

# Su-22M-1/M-3 Fitter H

During the mid-1970s, the Sukhoi OKB began development work on an improved variant of the Su-17 with an emphasis on improving the weapons load and overall performance. During the initial design work, the OKB suffered a setback when Pavel O. Sukhoi died on 15 September 1975. The administration of the OKB was turned over to three men, Y.E. Ivanov, Y.S. Felsner, and N.G. Zyrin, however, the name Sukhoi was retained to honor its founder, Pavel O. Sukhoi.

Although the new aircraft would retain the same basic fuselage and wing of the Su-17, it would feature an entirely new nose section. The redesigned nose was longer, deeper and was slightly drooped to improve pilot visibility over the nose. The Doppler radar antenna housing under the nose was deleted, and the radar was now housed in the deepened forward fuselage with a dielectric panel for the radar antenna mounted on the fuselage underside in front of the nosewheel doors. The upgraded Su-17 was powered by the 24,692 pound thrust Lyulka AL-21F-3 engine, giving it a maximum speed at low level of 1,367 mph.

The first prototype, designated the Su-22M, flew for the first time during 1977, and, after a lengthy test period, entered production some two years later under the designation Su-22M-1. Besides the entirely new nose section, the Su-22M differed in a number of ways from the earlier Su-17 Fitter C. The two-piece bulged nose wheel doors were replaced by single piece doors, similar to those used on the Su-7BM. The single retractable landing light under the nose was replaced by two retractable landing lights mounted on either side of the nose. The Odd Rods IFF antenna was repositioned from in front of the nose wheel doors to a new position behind the nosewheel well.

Improvements in the onboard avionics are revealed by the presence of dielectric panels on the underside of the nose for a radar altimeter in addition to the panel for the Doppler radar antenna. The laser rangefinder fitted to the Fitter C was replaced with a Laser Target Designator System (LTDS) mounted in the same centerbody shock cone location. The LTDS detects laser energy for an illuminated target (either by a ground based or airborne laser illuminator) and feeds range/bearing information directly into the fire control computer. The computer then automatically releases the selected weapons at the proper distance from the target. As part of the overall fire control computer sensor fit, a temperature probe was mounted on the port side of the fuselage below and in front of the cockpit.

To compensate for the increased nose area, the dorsal spine was enlarged, giving the fuselage a humped-back appearance, and the vertical fin leading edge was extended, blending into the dorsal spine at a raked angle, similar to the fin extension first used on the export Su-17M Fitter F. The vertical fin was also raised slightly and the fin tip was squared off and a removable ventral fin was installed on the fuselage underside behind the wing trailing edge.

The first Soviet Frontal Aviation regiments were re-equipped with the Su-22M-1 during 1980. These aircraft initially carried the same armament as the Su-17/20 series, however, they were soon cleared to carry the AS-7 Kerry, a tactical air-to-surface missile with a speed of Mach .6 and a range of seven miles. When configured with the AS-7, the Su-22M-1 is normally armed with a pair of K-13A/AA-2 Atoll air-to-air missiles on the outboard wing pylons for self defense. The increased load carrying capability of Su-22M-1 also allowed these aircraft to carry the UB-32 rocket pod, containing thirty-two S-5 57MM hollow charge air-to-ground unguided rockets.

The Su-22M-1 received the NATO reporting name Fitter H and is standard equipment for a number of first line Soviet Frontal Aviation units.

Late in the production life of the Su-22M-1, the aircraft was upgraded with improved avionics under the designation Su-22M-3. In addition to the avionics upgrades, an additional pylon was added to each wing between the wing root pylon and the outboard

**This early production Su-22M-1 Fitter H of a Soviet Frontal Aviation unit is armed with UB-32 thirty-two shot rocket pods on the fuselage pylons, AS-7 Kerry air-to-surface missiles on the inboard wing pylons, and K-13A (AA-2 Atoll) air-to-air missiles on the outboard wing pylons.**

pylon. These weapons pylons are dedicated to the carriage of air-to-air missiles, either the AA-2 Atoll or AA-8 Aphid.

Additionally, the Su-22M-3 has also been exported to Hungary, the sole non-Soviet user of this variant. Hungary has received approximately forty Su-22M-1s which are based at Taszár in southern Hungary, close to the Yugoslav border.

## Nose Development

**Su-22 Fitter F**



**Su-22M-1/3 Fitter H**

A pair of Su-22M-1s make a low pass over a Soviet T-72 tank during an exercise in the Magdeburg Area during March of 1987. Both aircraft are equipped with drop tanks on the outboard wing pylons and AS-7 Kerry air-to-surface missiles on the inboard wing pylons. Although the Fitter H remains in service with the Group of Soviet Forces Germany, it is being replaced by the more advanced Fitter K.

Red 14, an Su-22M-3 Fitter H of the Hungarian Air Force, departs from Taszár Air Base for another training sortie loaded with UB-32 rocket pods on each inboard wing pylon and 158 gallon drop tanks on the fuselage pylons.

## Fuselage Development

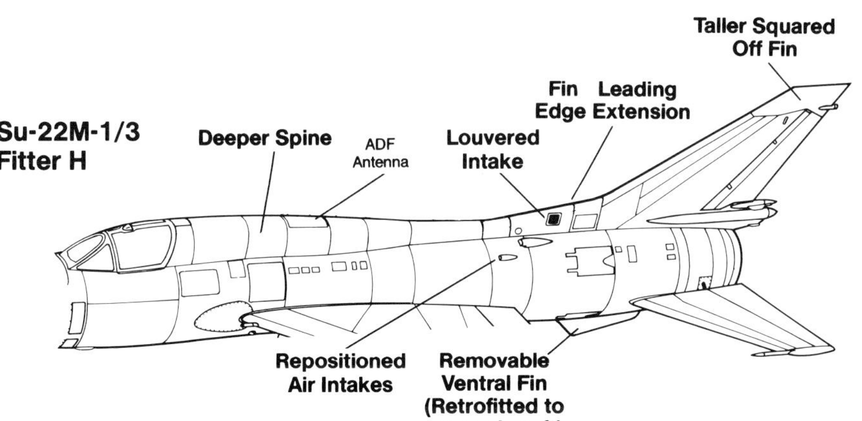



This Su-22M-3 Fitter H was one of forty delivered to the Hungarian Air Force, the first Warsaw Pact nation to receive the Su-22. The Fitter has been retrofitted with an air-to-air missile pylon on the wing and carries a missile rail on the inboard wing plyon which can accomodate either an AA-2 Atoll or AS-7 Kerry missile.

Red 32, an Su-22M-1 Fitter H of a Soviet Frontal Aviation unit taxies out for another mission armed with a UB-32 rocket pod on each outer wing pylon. This Fitter H is an early production Su-22 retrofitted with a third wing pylon for an air-to-air missile (usually a K-60/AA-8 Aphid) on the wing inboard of the first wing fence.

Soviet flight line personnel position a tow bar under the nose of a Soviet Air Force Fitter H. The air data boom sensors are covered to prevent them from damage. The Fitters carry different styles of tactical numbers; Red 77 is outlined in White while Red 56 has no outline, and an early style air intake warning triangle. The color of the tactical number within a Soviet regiment usually denotes the squadron within the regiment.

The deeper nose section of the Fitter H houses a Doppler radar antenna internally. The small blade antenna on the underside of the nose is the antenna for the radio altimeter and the small blister fairing on the portside of the nose is for the angle-of-attack sensor vane.

# Su-22M-2 Fitter J

To meet the needs of its many client states, the Soviets have developed an export variant of the Su-22M-1 under the designation Su-22M-2. The primary difference between the Su-22M-1 and Su-22M-2 was the powerplant used and the electronics suite installed in the aircraft. The Su-22M-2 is powered by a 25,350 pound thrust Tumansky R-29B engine in place of the Lyulka AL-21F-3 engine used in the Su-22M-1. This engine is the same as that installed in the MiG-23/27 Flogger series and there is some speculation that the decision to use the Tumansky engine on the export Su-22M-2 was made in order to make these aircraft compatible with the MiG-23s in service with many Soviet client states. With both aircraft powered by the same engine, maintenance and supply problems for the client states would be greatly simplified. Installation of the Tumansky engine resulted in a slightly recontoured rear fuselage, which is bulged to accommodate the larger diameter of the Tumansky engine.

Most Su-22M-2s also carry a downgraded electronics suite when compared to the standard first line Soviet Su-22M-1. It is believed that the majority of Su-22M-2s do not carry the LTDS, however, they may be equipped with a laser rangefinder. The export Su-22M-2 received the NATO reporting name Fitter J and has been sold to Angola, Libya, Peru, the Peoples Democratic Republic of Yemen (PDRY), and the Yemen Arab Republic (YAR). The Libyans have made use of their Fitter Js in both the ground attack and air defense roles. When configured for air defense, Fitter Js normally carry two 250 gallon drop tanks on the outer wing pylons and a pair of AA-2 Atoll air-to-air missiles on the inboard wing pylons.

On 19 August 1981 two of Colonel Muammar el-Gadaffi's Su-22M-2 Fitter Js attacked two U.S. Navy F-14A Tomcats from the carrier USS Nimitz over the Gulf of Sidra. The Gulf, according to international maritime law, was international waters, however, Gadaffi had claimed this part of the Mediterranean Sea as Libyan territorial water. The AA-2 Atoll fired by the lead Fitter missed the two Tomcats of VF-41 Black Aces. The lead Tomcat was flown by CDR Henry Kleemann with his RIO LT Dave Venlet, while his wingman was LT Larry Muczynski with LT Jim Anderson as his RIO. Once fired upon, the Americans did not hesitate to defend themselves and engaged the Fitters. After a short maneuvering fight over the Mediterranean Sea, the two Tomcat pilots each locked on to a Fitter with an AIM-9L Sidewinder air-to-air missile. Both Fitters were hit, and although both pilots ejected, only one parachute was seen to open. In a few short minutes, the Sukhoi Su-22 had earned the doubtful distinction of being the loser in the first engagement between variable geometry winged fighters.

**An early production Su-22M-2 Fitter J of the Peoples Democratic Republic of Yemen Air Force (PDRYAF). Export Fitter Js lack much of the advanced avionics equipment that is carried by Warsaw Pact Su-22M-1/3 Fitter H and Su-22M-4 Fitter K strike fighters.**

**A Libyan Arab Air Force (LAAF) Fitter J flies a surveillance mission over the Gulf of Sidra armed with four AA-2 Atoll air-to-air missiles. Libyan Fitters are often used in the air defense role, supplimenting the MiG-23s and Mirage F-1s in missions over the Gulf.**

## Engine Development

**Su-22M-1 Fitter H**

**Su-22M-2**

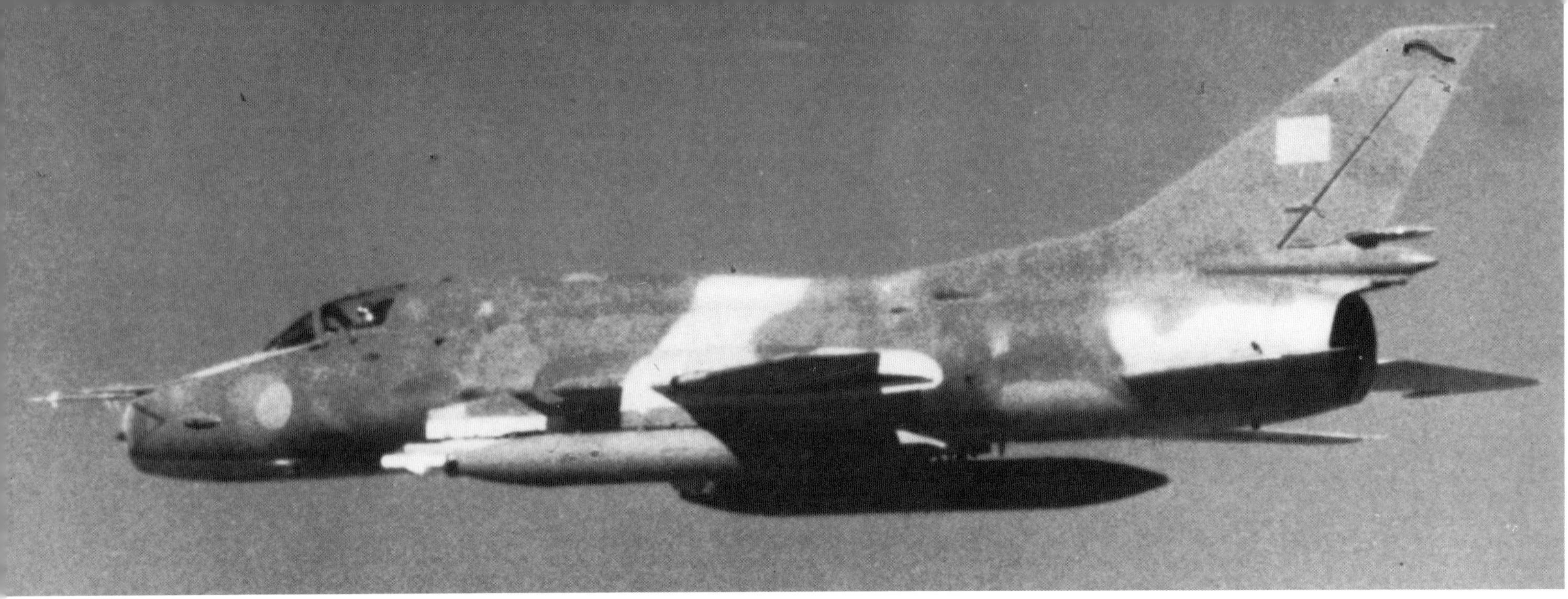

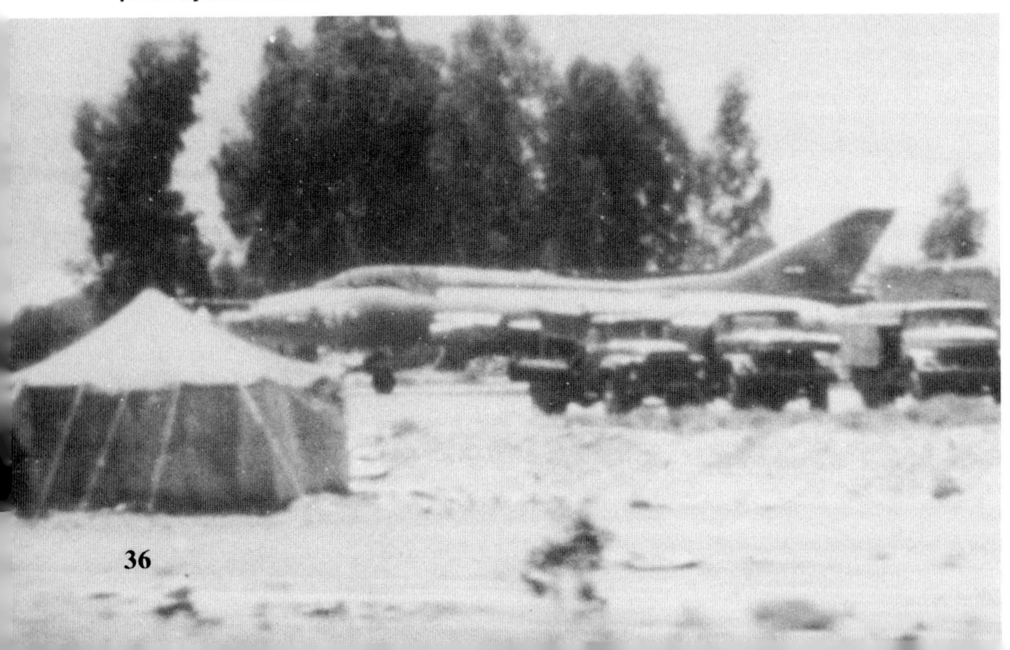

An LAAF Fitter J over the Mediterranean Sea during August of 1981. Two such aircraft were shot down by U.S. Navy F-14A Tomcats of VF-41 aboard USS NIMITZ when the lead Fitter fired an AA-2 Atoll at the Tomcats.

An Su-22M-2 Fitter J of the Yemen Arab Republic Air Force parked on the ramp at its home base. Both North and South Yemen fly the Fitter J and the training given their pilots by Soviet instructors is reportedly limited, contrasting sharply with the training given North Yemeni F-5 pilots by American instructors.

## Missile Armament

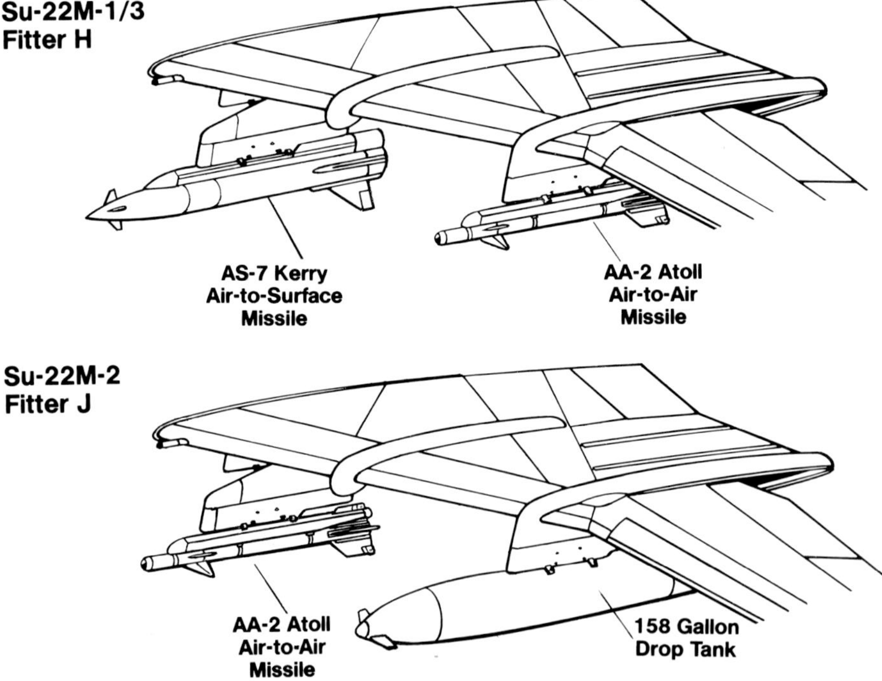

# Su-22M-4 Fitter K

After a relatively small number of Su-22M-1/M-3 Fitter Hs were produced, Sukhoi shifted production to an improved variant designated the Su-22M-4. Production Su-22M-4s first appeared during 1985 and were given the NATO reporting name Fitter K. The Fitter K remains the current production variant, both for Warsaw Pact use and for export.

The Su-22M-4 featured a number of improvements over the Su-22M-2/M-3 Fitter H series. To increase cooling for the afterburner liner, a ram air intake was added to the fin leading edge extension above the dorsal spine. Immediately above this cooling air intake is a small unidentified antenna or probe. The two smaller cooling ram air inlets on the fuselage were enlarged, repositioned, and a third intake was added to the fuselage. To increase low-level stability, a small removable ventral fin was added to the underside of the rear fuselage, below the air brakes (this ventral fin has been retrofitted to a number of earlier Fitter H and J aircraft.)

To accommodate an air-to-air missile (AAM), a dedicated AAM pylon was added between the wing root pylon and the outboard pylon. It is believed this pylon is capable of carrying either an AA-2 Atoll or an AA-8 Aphid (this pylon has been retrofitted to many of the earlier Su-22M-1 Fitter H and Su-22M-2 Fitter J series aircraft). The AA-2 Atoll is a first generation Soviet air-to-air missile with both infrared homing and radar guided versions. The missile has a range of four miles. The AA-8 Aphid (Soviet designation K-60) is a newer missile and is a highly maneuverable close range solid propellant weapon with infrared homing guidance, a 13.2 pound warhead, and a range of 4.3 miles.

The Su-22M-4 is fitted with the KM-1 zero/zero rocket powered ejection seat which is capable of boosting the pilot to an altitude of 150 feet in the case of a ground-level ejection. The seat carries an improved Type NAZ-7 survival kit in the seat headrest, which contains both a survival kit and a inflatable rubber raft. In the event of an ejection, the kit is deployed after the pilot separates from the seat and is suspended below the pilot by a long wire. The KM-1/NAZ-7 combination is being retrofitted to most Su-22M-1/3s and M-2s.

The Su-22M-4 is cleared to carry a large variety of weapons such as Type S-24 240MM aircraft rockets, FAB 100, 200, 500, and 1000 kg bombs, PTAB anti-personnel bomblet dispensers, SOV-AB chemical weapons tanks/dispensers, GSh-23L 23MM gun pods, and 158 gallon drop tanks. Recently a multiple ejector type bomb rack has been identified on Warsaw Pact Su-22M-4s. This rack is capable of carrying six FAB 100 kg bombs. The Su-22M-4 can also be equipped with chaff/flare dispenser pods mounted on rails attached to the upper fuselage near the tail. Most Fitter K aircraft carry two such pods, however, a number of aircraft have been noted carrying four pods, again this rack/pod combination is being retrofitted to earlier Fitter variants.

For precision attacks against high value targets in heavily defended airspace, the Su-22M-4 can carry a number of stand-off air-to-surface guided missiles. Besides the earlier AS-7 Kerry missile, the Su-22M-4 is capable of carrying several new generation Soviet tactical air-to-surface weapons. These include the AS-10 Karen and AS-14 Kedge. The AS-10 is a semi-active laser homing weapon with a speed of Mach .8 and a range of six miles. The AS-14 is a thirteen-foot missile with a range of some twenty-five mile, it is also believed to be a laser semi-active homing missile.

In addition to the air-to-surface missile capability, it is believed that the Su-22M-4 can carry Laser Guided Bombs (LGBs), similar to the American Paveway series of LGBs used in Vietnam. These weapons home on reflected laser energy from targets that have been illuminated by either ground units or another aircraft equipped with a laser illuminator. The bombs are released in either a shallow dive or in a loft maneuver. A new

Red 362 (The 3 has been overpainted) of the *Luftstreitkrafte* (East German Air Force) taxies out armed with UB-32 rocket pods on the inboard wing pylons. The UB-32 carries thirty-two Type S-5 57MM unguided air-to-ground rockets. A Red Tactical Number on an East German Air Force aircraft identifies the aircraft as being assigned to a combat unit.

A Polish Air Force Fitter K rolls out after landing with its drag chute fully deployed. Shortly before the aircraft comes to a complete halt, the drag chute will be detached by the pilot for recovery by the ground crew.

generation of Soviet Laser Guided Bombs is expected to enter service in the near future and the Su-22M-4 Fitter K will most likely be cleared to carry these weapons as well.

The Fitter K can also be configured for tactical nuclear strike with the TN-1000 or TN-1200 tactical nuclear bombs. For such missions, the Su-22M-4 would most likely be configured with the weapon on the port inboard pylon and four 211 gallon drop tanks on the outboard wing stations and fuselage stations. For self protection up to three air-to-air missiles could be carried as well.

Another weapon used on the Su-22M-4 is the Fuel/Air Explosive (FAE) tank, which resembles a large fuel drop tank. These weapons have been used in combat in Afghanistan with devastating effect. The FAE is used primarily to attack large area targets (such as troop concentrations, airfields, or villages) and has a lethal radius of up to 1,300 feet. The weapon produces a huge fire-ball and kills either by fire, burning off the oxygen in the air, or from the tremendous over-pressure caused by the blast. It is estimated that the Su-22M-4 can carry four to six of these tanks on the fuselage and underwing pylons.

The first Warsaw Pact country to receive the Fitter K was Poland which took delivery of their first aircraft during 1985. There are currently ninety Fitter Ks based at Pila and Smardazko. During the Summer of 1985 the German Democratic Republic received ninety Fitter Ks which are based at Laage. There are two units equipped with the Fitter K, *Marineflieger Gechwader* 28 of the East German Naval Air Force and *Jagdbombenfliegeschawader* 32 (Fighter Bomber Regiment 32), also known as the *Gebhard Leberecht von Blücher* regiment.

The Czech Air Force also has received the Fitter K, having received the first of forty-five Su-22M-4 Fitter K and Su-22U Fitter G aircraft during 1985. These aircraft are currently based at Bechyne as part of the 10th Tactical Division. Interestingly, all the Fitters sold to Poland, East Germany, and Czechoslovakia were delivered in crates and reassembled by Soviet specialists. After assembly they were flight tested by a factory test pilot before the Fitters were offically turned over to their new owners.

For the tactical reconnaissance role, the Su-22M-4 can also carry the standard twenty-one foot photographic/ELINT pod on the fuselage centerline. This pod contains

**This Polish Fitter K, Red 3911, is unusual in that it has the tactical number on the nose outlined in White. Normally only training aircraft, such as Su-22U Fitter Gs, have White outlined tactical numbers. This Fitter is armed with UB-32 rocket pods on the wing pylons and FAB 100 bombs on the fuselage pylons.**

**A Polish Fitter K is parked in front of its hardened aircraft shelter on a Polish air base. Normally when the Fitter K is parked, the wings are kept in the fully swept position to save space and to allow the aircraft to be easily maneuvered into and out of its shelter.**

The Fitter K carries landing lights on both main landing gear legs and on the nosewheel leg. The lights on the wingtips are position lights for night formation flying.

forward looking, oblique, and vertical cameras, as well as photo flash cartridges for night operations. On the sides of the pod are dielectric panels for the ELINT antennas.

The Su-22M-4 is expected to remain in service well into the 1990s and will steadily replace the Su-7 and Su-17 as the most important ground-attack aircraft in the Warsaw Pact.

## Fuselage Development

### Su-22M-1/3 Fitter H

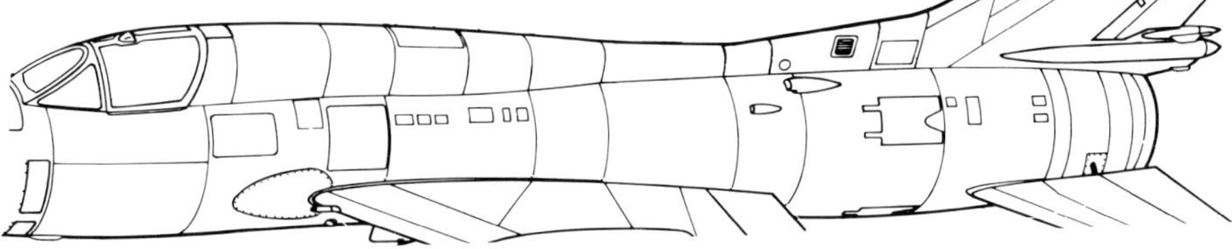

### Su-22M-4 Fitter K

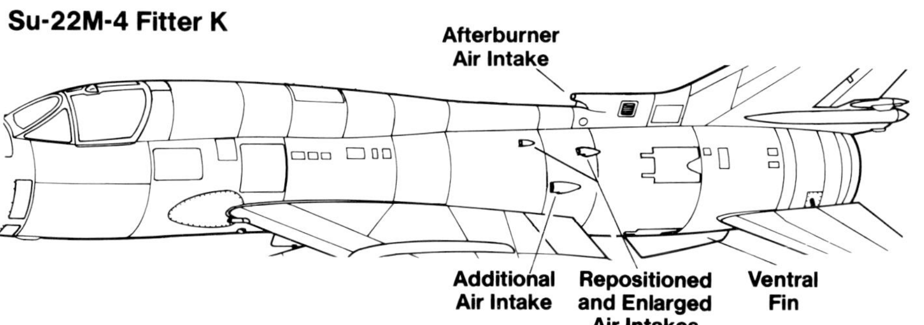

A pair of Soviet Frontal Aviation Fitter Ks assigned to the Group of Soviet Forces Germany fly formation during early 1987. Both aircraft are configured for long range cruise with the wings swept forward and 158 gallon drop tanks on the fuselage pylons.

A pair of *Luftstreitkrafte* Su-22M-4 Fitter Ks take off with 158 gallon drop tanks on the outboard wing pylons and either chemical tanks or napalm bombs on the fuselage pylons. The Fitter K can carry either weapon.

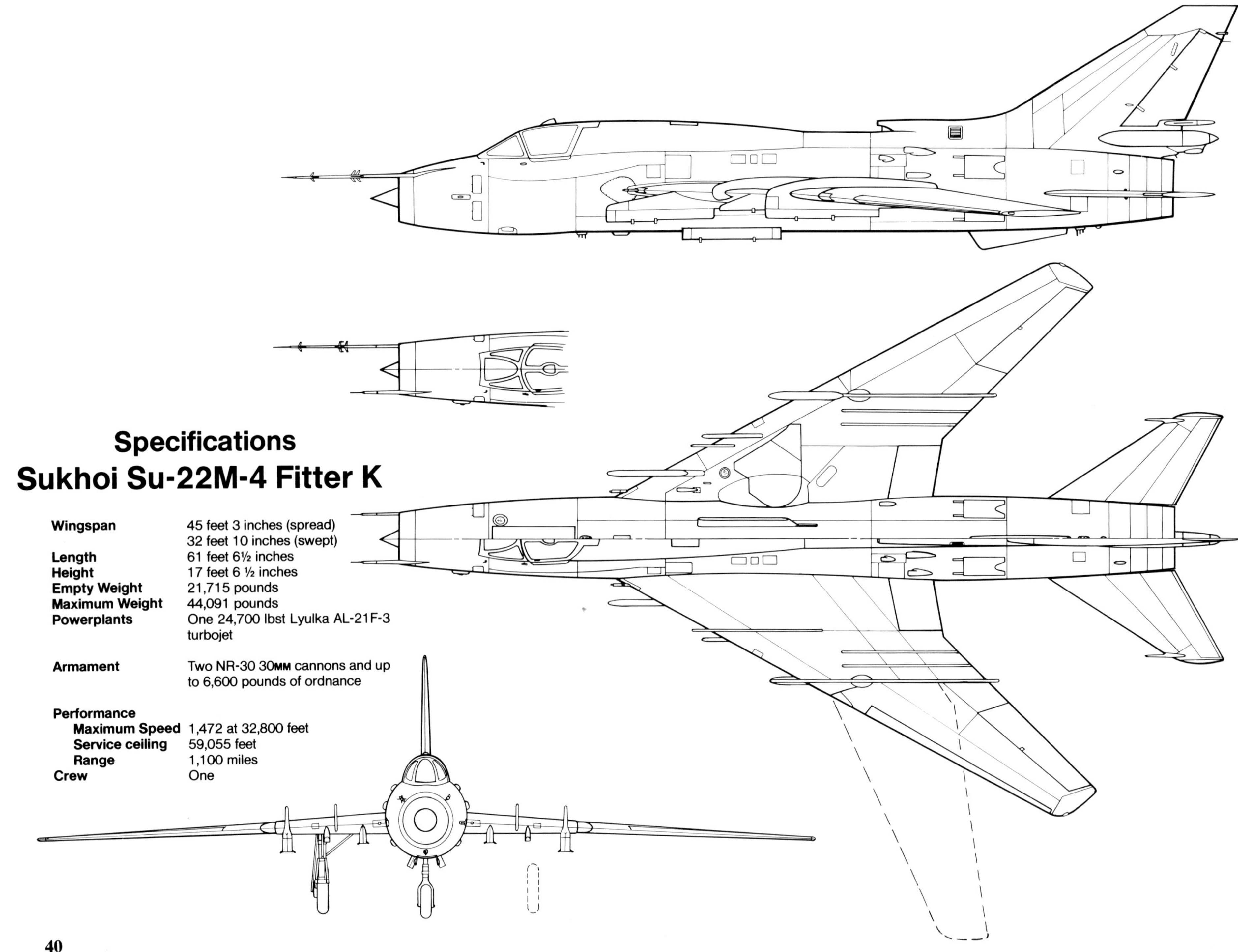

Specifications
Sukhoi Su-22M-4 Fitter K

Wingspan        45 feet 3 inches (spread)
                32 feet 10 inches (swept)
Length          61 feet 6½ inches
Height          17 feet 6 ½ inches
Empty Weight    21,715 pounds
Maximum Weight  44,091 pounds
Powerplants     One 24,700 lbst Lyulka AL-21F-3
                turbojet

Armament        Two NR-30 30мм cannons and up
                to 6,600 pounds of ordnance

Performance
  Maximum Speed 1,472 at 32,800 feet
  Service ceiling 59,055 feet
  Range         1,100 miles
Crew            One

Armorers load belted 30ᴍᴍ rounds into the fuselage ammunition storage bin of a Polish Air Force Su-22M-4 Fitter K. The inscription on the UB-32 rocket pod in the foreground is in Russian, not Polish.

## Wing Pylons

**Su-22M-1/3 Fitter H**

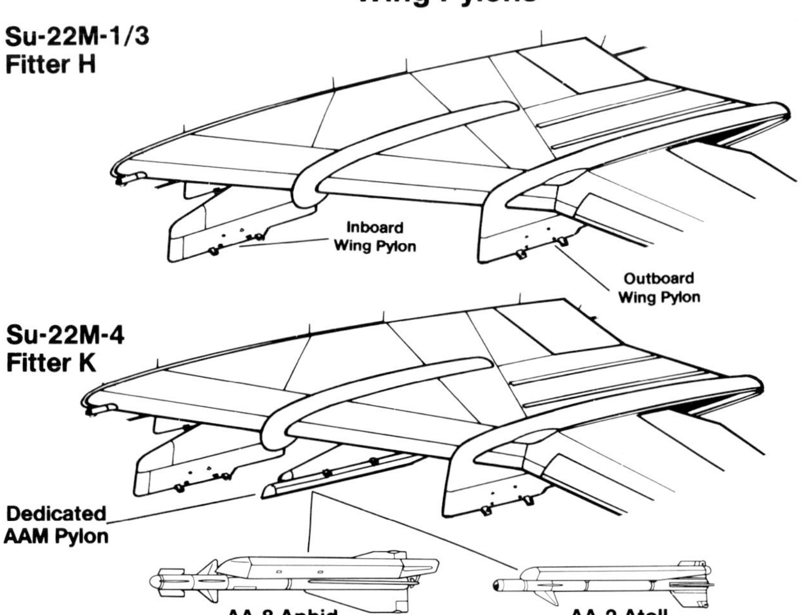



**Su-22M-4 Fitter K**

A ground crew checks the balance of the nose wheel tire of an Su-22M-4 Fitter K of the Polish Air Force. The dedicated AAM wing plyon missile rack is capable of carrying either the AA-2 Atoll or AA-8 Aphid air-to-air missile.

Red 45, an Su-22M-4 Fitter K of the *Luftstreitkrafte* taxies out loaded with eight UB-32 rocket pods and a pair of K-60 (AA-8 Aphid) air-to-air missiles. The MiG-23BN (Flogger F) taking off behind it is one of East Germany's latest acquisitions, assigned to *Jagdbombergeschwader 31 Klement Gottwald*, at Holzdorf.

A Polish Air Force Su-22M-4 Fitter K is towed to its parking spot by a fuel truck. The ground crewman walking alongside the aircraft is a safety spotter, while the man in the cockpit controls the aircraft's brakes.

This Polish Air Force Su-22M-4 Fitter K carries four chaff/flare dispenser tubes on the paired upper fuselage racks, which are visible just above the first wing fence.

## Fitter Armament

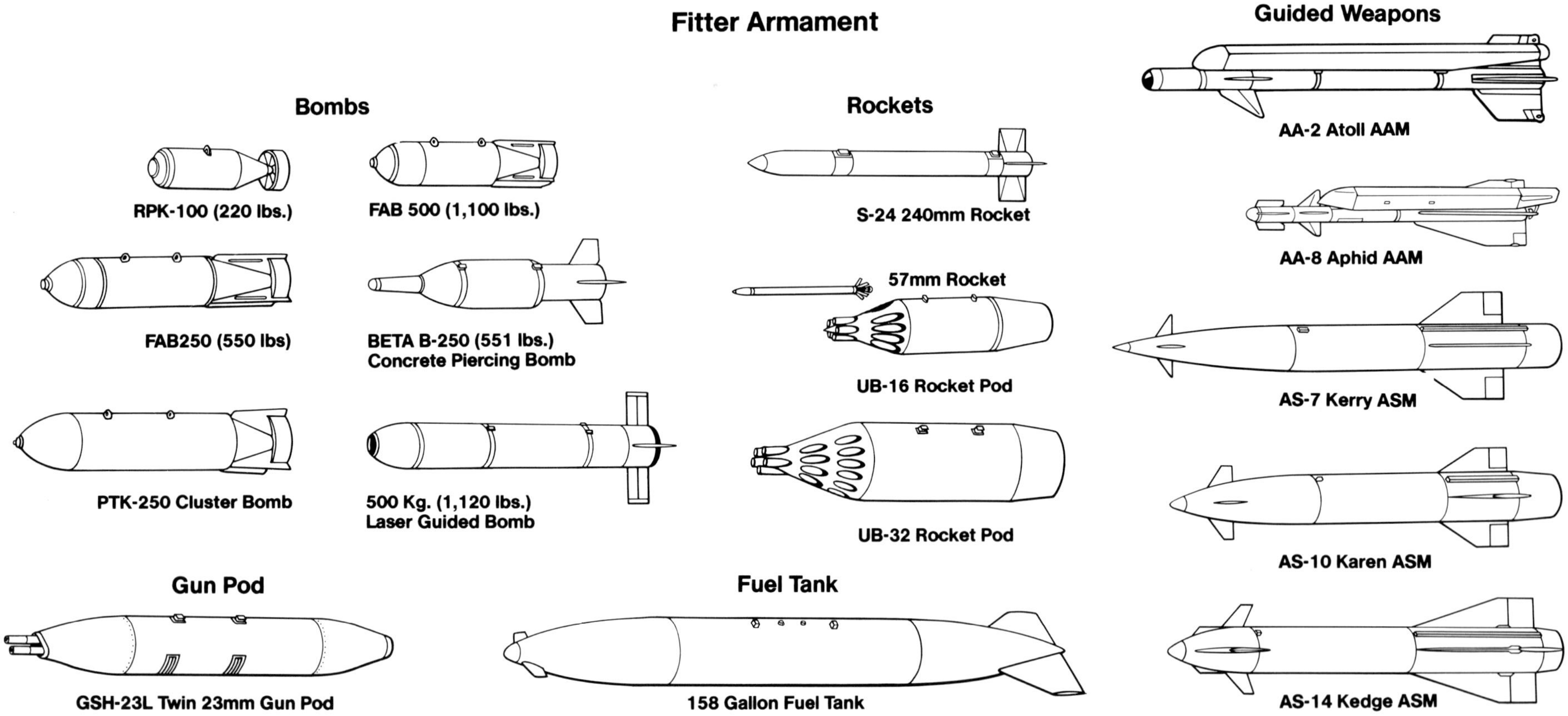

### Bombs

RPK-100 (220 lbs.)

FAB 500 (1,100 lbs.)

FAB250 (550 lbs)

BETA B-250 (551 lbs.)
Concrete Piercing Bomb

PTK-250 Cluster Bomb

500 Kg. (1,120 lbs.)
Laser Guided Bomb

### Gun Pod

GSH-23L Twin 23mm Gun Pod

### Rockets

S-24 240mm Rocket

57mm Rocket

UB-16 Rocket Pod

UB-32 Rocket Pod

### Fuel Tank

158 Gallon Fuel Tank

### Guided Weapons

AA-2 Atoll AAM

AA-8 Aphid AAM

AS-7 Kerry ASM

AS-10 Karen ASM

AS-14 Kedge ASM

A flight of four Polish Fitter Ks fly in combat spread formation. The lead Fitter K is configured with four fuselage plyons, while the others carry only two pylons. The second element leader is equipped with chaff/flare dispenser racks on the upper fuselage on either side of the fuselage spine.

## Multiple Bomb Rack
### (Six FAB 100 (220 lbs.) Bombs)

**Su-22M-4**

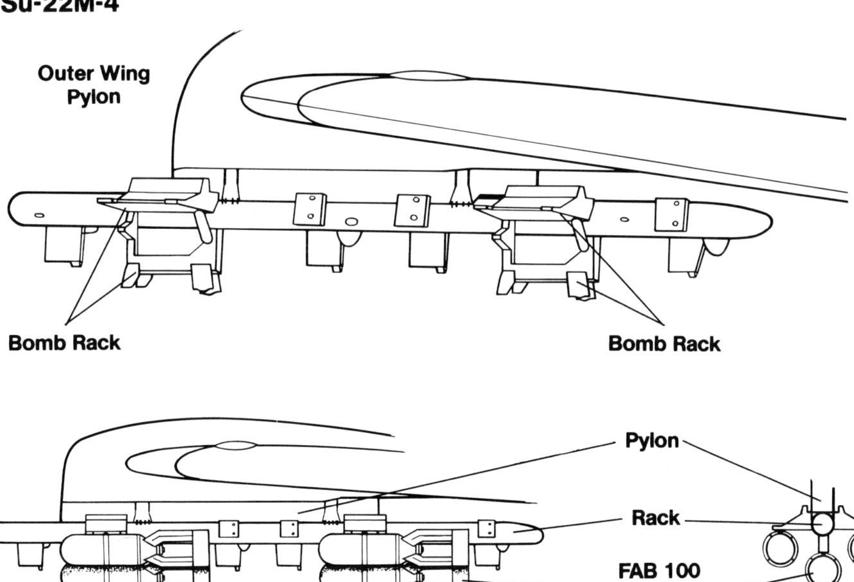

An East German Air Force Su-22M-4 Fitter K takes off from Holzdorf on 29 August 1985. The aircraft carries multiple ejector bomb racks on the outboard wing pylons and chaff/flare dispenser racks on the fuselage sides on either side of the vertical stabilizer.

Red 23, a Fitter K of the German Democratic Republic Air Force prepares for another sortie from Holzdorf Air Base. The aircraft is equipped with multiple ejector bomb racks capable of carrying six FAB 100 bombs on both the outer and inner wing plyons. The Fitters are normally based at Laage Air Base.

Red 3204 of the Polish Air Force is equipped with four paired fuselage racks for chaff/flare dispensers. In combat, each pair of racks would be configured with a single chaff/flare dispenser to give the Fitter protection against enemy radars and surface-to-air missiles.

A Polish Air Force Su-22M-4 Fitter K parked on a rain-soaked ramp of a Polish Air Force base. The Fitter K is the most modern attack aircraft in the inventory of the Polish Air Force and forms the backbone of the tactical fighter force.

Ground crews conduct maintenance work on a Polish Fitter K. The intake screens around the nose and blow-in doors are designed to protect the ground crews during ground engine run-ups and to protect the engine from foreign object damage (FOD).

## Fuselage Chaff/Flare Dispenser Racks

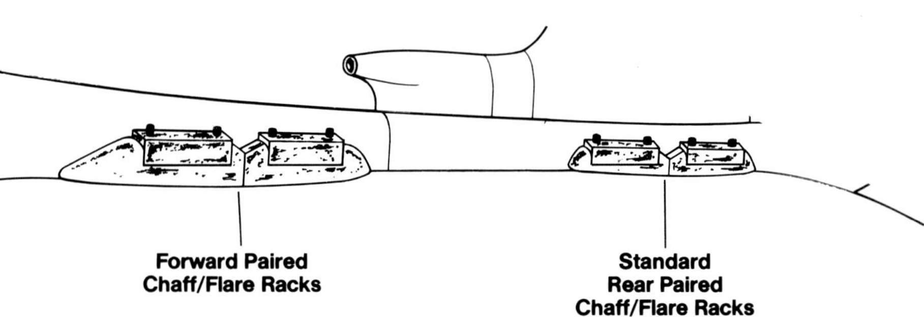

Polish soldiers dressed in anti-chemical warfare protective coveralls and masks guard a line of Su-22M-4 Fitter Ks. The antenna for the Sirena 3 radar warning system is mounted just above the drag chute housing and provides rear radar detection and warning.

Polish ground crew check the instrument air data probe on a Polish Air Force Su-22M-4 Fitter K with testing equipment made in West Germany. The use of Western equipment in Warsaw Pact forces is not that unusual. During the late 1950s, Czech built MiG-15s and Il-10s were equipped with Swiss-made clocks.

A Soviet crew chief instructs the ground crew of Blue 06, a Fitter K of a Frontal Aviation Guards Regiment on their duties for the day. The Guards' emblem is carried on the fuselage just behind the White outlined stencil style Blue aircraft tactical number.

While the rest of his flight waits for him, a Polish Air Force pilot deplanes from his Su-22M-4 Fitter K after another practice mission. The aircraft is configured with four under-fuselage weapons plyons instead of the usual two pylons.

# Su-22U Fitter E/G

A two-seat trainer, based on the Su-22M-1 Fitter H airframe, was developed to aid pilots in transition to the variable geometry variants of the Fitter. There had been no such trainer version for the earlier Su-17 Fitter C and pilots had to convert directly from the fixed wing Su-7U Moujik to the Su-17. The Su-22U was developed in order to improve the training cycle and reduce the accident rate among pilots transitioning from fixed wing aircraft to the variable geometry Fitters. Although the trainer went into production during the same time frame as the Su-22M-1 Fitter H, it was observed by NATO before the single-seat fighter and therefore received an earlier NATO Reporting Name, Fitter E.

The Fitter E differs from the single-seat Su-22M-1 in having a second cockpit for an instructor pilot installed in the fuselage in place of the fuselage fuel tank. To improve forward visibility for the instructor, a retractable periscope/mirror was added on top of the canopy and the rear view mirror on the front canopy was deleted. Additionally, the portside NR-30 cannon was deleted, however, the Fitter E carries the same avionics, the same number of ordnance pylons, and can use the same weapons as the single-seat Su-22M-1 Fitter H, making the trainer fully combat capable.

Su-22Us exported to foreign customers outside of the Warsaw Pact are powered by the Tumansky R-29B engine in place of the Lyuka Al-21F-3 engine (the NATO Reporting Name reflects no difference between a Tumansky or a Lyulka powered Su-22U, both being known as the Fitter E). Tumansky-powered Fitter Es have been exported to Afghanistan, Angola, Iraq, Libya, Syria, South Yemen, North Yemen, Vietnam, and Peru.

An improved variant (believed to be based on the Su-22M-4 airframe), followed the Su-22U on the production line. This improved Su-22U featured the taller squared off vertical tail and ventral fin of the Su-22M-4, although the fin intake and dedicated AAM pylon were not installed. Su-22Us can be equipped with single chaff/flare dispensers on either side of the tail, while the single seat Su-22M-4 can carry two such dispensers. These aircraft have been given the NATO reporting name Fitter G. The Fitter G has become the standard Fitter trainer variant in use with Warsaw Pact forces.

A number of Warsaw Pact air forces use special markings on trainer aircraft to denote their role as trainers. Polish Fitter Gs carry a three digit number on the nose outlined in white, while the Polish Fitter K fighters carry a four digit unoutlined number. Fitter Gs assigned to the *Luftstreitkrafte* (German Democratic Republic Air Force) have black tac-

An East German Su-22U takes off from Laage Air Base for a training mission with the landing lights and rear cockpit periscope/mirror system deployed.

Red 65 is an early production Su-22U Fitter E of the Soviet Air Force. Few Su-22Us were delivered in natural metal finish, most were delivered from the factory in a tactical camouflage paint scheme.

tical numbers which identifies them as trainer aircraft (or an aircraft assigned to a training unit). Fitter Ks carry a red number, which denotes assignment to a combat unit.

The Soviet Air Force does not use the tactical number or special markings to identify trainers. The tactical number on the nose of a Soviet Air Force Fitter consists of the last two or three digits of the aircraft serial number and the color usually identifies either the aircraft's regiment or squadron.

Red 307, a Polish Air Force Su-22U Fitter G returns from a training mission with a single FAB 100 bomb on the starboard fuselage pylon. Used primarly as a proficiency and conversion trainer, the Su-22U has the same internal equipment and avionics as the single-seat Fitter K.

"

An Su-22U Fitter G of the Polish Air Force is parked on its rain-soaked hardstand at a Polish Air Force Base. This Fitter trainer carries a single, paired upper fuselage chaff/flare rack on either side of the vertical stabilizer, instead of the two paired racks found on the Su-22M-4 Fitter K.

A student and his instructor prepare for a training mission in an Su-22U Fitter G. The two White bars on the upper rear canopy frame are the controls for the periscope/mirror system. The Fitter G also has a multi-panel window separating the two cockpits, with one of the panels being visible behind the students ejection seat.

An Su-22U Fitter G prepares to taxi out on another training mission. The boom in the foreground is part of an underground refueling system in use at this Polish Air Force base. The boom can swivel through 360 degrees to service aircraft parked on either side of the boom.

## Nose Development

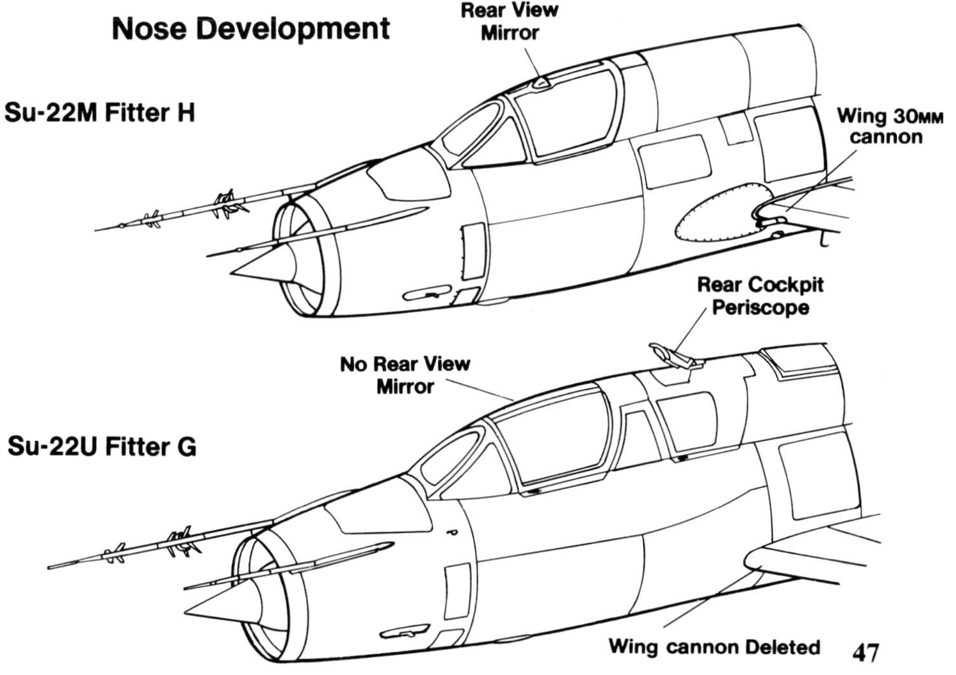

The Fitter G is used to train pilots on all variants of the swing-wing Fitter, including these earlier Su-20 Fitter Cs of the Polish Air Force. The tactical number is Red outlined in White, while the tactical numbers on the natural metal Su-20s are Red with no outline.

A Polish Air Force pilot in the cockpit of an Su-22M-4 Fitter K. All lettering in the cockpit is in Cyrilic, the Russian alphabet. The cockpit is painted in Chromate Green, while the gunsight is in Black. The center button on the stick is in Red and is the emergency jettison button that jettisons all external stores.

The boarding ladder for the Fitter G features an extended platform for use by the instructor pilot. The two harnesses hanging from the inboard weapons plyon of Red 307 are the parachute harnesses for the instructor and student.

A Polish Air Force Su-22U Fitter G taxies in from another training mission. The drag chute housing is open and this aircraft is outfitted with four chaff/flare dispenser racks on the upper fuselage sides.

While his student waits on the ground, a Polish Air Force instructor pilot deplanes from this Su-22U Fitter G. The pointed object on the ground at the left is the air intake cover plate which will be be installed over the intake shock cone, completely sealing off the air intake.

An Su-22U Fitter G taxies out to begin another training mission. The Fitter G trainer does not carry the dedicated AAM wing plyon and has the port NR-30 cannon removed, however, the aircraft can have the same weapons as the single-seat fighter and is fully combat capable.

This Polish Air Force Su-22U is configured with chaff/flare dispenser racks on the rear fuselage on either side of the vertical stabilizer. The two-seat Su-22U is a fully combat capable trainer and carries the same weapon loads as the single seat Fitter K (with the exception of the dedicated AAM wing pylon).

Su-22U Fitter Gs parked on the flight line of a Polish Air Force base. The generator in the foreground supplies external electrical power to the aircraft for instrument checks, radio checks, and to start the aircraft.

# Jet Fighters in Action

**1024**

**1032**

**1053**

**1058**

**1065**

**1070**

 **squadron/signal publications**